Home Baked
Family Favorites
with frozen dough

Rhodes Bake-N-Serv™
Salt Lake City, Utah

ISBN (10): 0-61540-346-8
ISBN (13): 978-0-615-40346-5

Printed in the United States of America
First Printing 2010

Editors: Sue Petersen, Jenna Jackson,
    Whitney Olsen, Kenny Farnsworth

Editorial Assistants: Carrie Whiting, Robyn Dimond

Design: Mitchell Rogers, Dane Beck

Photography: Mitchell Rogers

Food and Set Stylist: Jenna Jackson

Test Kitchen: Julie Tolman, Sue Petersen

All of us at Rhodes Bake-N-Serv are dedicated to
providing you with fresh, reliable ideas to create
delicious homemade foods.

We welcome your comments and suggestions at:

RhodesBread.com

No-Fault Guarantee
If for any reason our product does not meet your
expectations, write us, or call toll-free

1-800-876-7333

We will send you a coupon of equivalent value and
make every effort to correct the problem in the future.

YES! You can successfully bake with Rhodes dough.
Let us show you how!

Call 1-800-876-7333 between 8AM – 5PM MST
and speak with a live customer satisfaction person.
Or, visit our website at www.rhodesbread.com for
baking tips and easy recipes for every occasion.

In Memory of Zoe Ann Farnsworth

Whitney Olsen
Chef, Recipe Development
Technical Editor

...zy, she can cook. Really well.
...t writing, reading, family and
...e outdoors are important, too.

...am & Parmesan Rolls, 21
...ple Fritters, 36
...lian Kaleidoscope Breadsticks, 64
...rk & Pineapple Pizza, 93
...uffed Crust Pizza, 96
...d Onion Focaccia, 98
...jun Crab Salad, 109
...aided Athenian Bread, 121
...uthern Peach Cobbler, 142
...awaiian Sweet Pizza, 146
...nanas Foster Medallions, 147

...ie Petersen
...edia Relations/Food, Photo Prep

...ves to sew and scrapbook. And travel.
...d spend a lot of time with the grandkids.

...ench Toast Sticks, 38
...eadstick Blossoms, 66
...scan Tomato Tart, 86
...nna-Bunnies, 180

...obyn Reading
...edia Relations Assistant

...ays handcrafting quilts, she's also
...a green thumb out in the backyard.

...entine Dinner Rolls, 178
...cky Dinner Rolls, 181
...ster Egg Dinner Rolls, 182
...cked Witch Dippers, 190

Diane Reeder
Retired

Fruit, vegetable gardener
and accomplished cook.

French Toast Pockets, 28

Mitch Rogers
Graphic Designer & Photographer

Toy collector, family man, avid cook
who's not afraid to bring the heat.

Cheesy Potato Chip Breadsticks, 74
Smiley Face Pizza, 82
Buffalo Chicken Pizza, 84
Fresh Fruit Pizza, 140
Almond Cream Cheese Squares, 159

Julie Tolman
Customer Satisfaction Manager
Food/Photo Preparation

Fond of hanging with the family and traveling,
she's also kind of funny.

Italian Panini, 124

Heidi VanValkenburg
Chief Product Demonstrator

Confirmed people-pleaser, do-gooder and
tireless cook of anything—at any time.

Twisty Buttery Breadsticks, 72

Scott VanValkenburg
Marketing

Crazy for camping, basketball
and playing board games.

Italian Deep Dish Pizza, 99
Churros, 151

Dave Wheeler
Regional Sales Manager

Skipper of the family sailboat crew,
and a bike rider.

Cinnamon Marble Loaf French Toast, 40

Scott Wheeler
IT Director

Woodworker, yardscaper, kayaker,
he's a big soccer fan. "Go Spain."

Braided Spaghetti Bread, 132

Carrie Whiting
Customer Satisfaction/
Media Relations

Time outdoors is gold. Cycling,
boating, making new friends,
she's a baker and chocolate fiend.

Hot Diggity Dogs, 107
Spinach Braid, 108
Baked Hot Dogs on a Stick, 110
Pumpkin Pear Bread Pudding, 164
Banana Nut Bread Pudding, 173

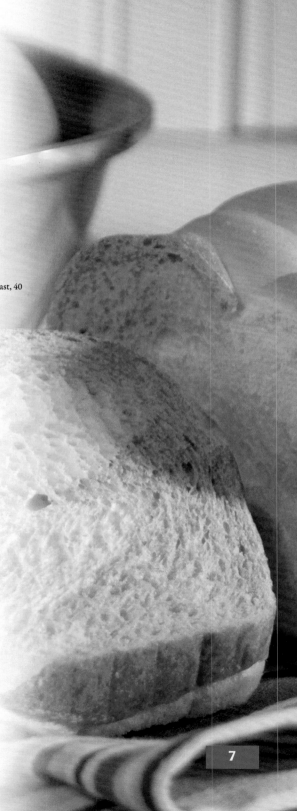

Parkerhouse Rolls

20 Rhodes™ Dinner Rolls, thawed but still cold
2 tablespoons butter or margarine, melted
flour

Using a little flour to prevent sticking, flatten each roll into an oval. Brush center with melted butter. Fold in half, pressing edges together slightly.

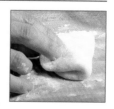

Dust top with flour and place on large sprayed baking sheet. Cover with sprayed plastic wrap and let rise until double in size. Remove wrap and bake at 350°F 15 - 20 minutes.

Kaiser Rolls

12 Rhodes Texas™ Rolls, thawed but still cold
1 egg, beaten
sesame or poppy seeds, if desired

Combine two rolls and roll into a 12-inch rope. Tie each rope into an overhand knot. Bring one end of the dough over the top and tuck down into the middle. Bring the other end of the dough through the center, going the opposite way. Place on a large sprayed baking sheet. If desired, brush with egg and sprinkle with sesame or poppy seeds. Cover with sprayed plastic wrap and let rise until double in size. Remove wrap and bake at 350°F 15-20 minutes.

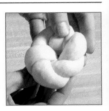

Butterflake Rolls

12 Rhodes Texas™ Rolls or 24 Rhodes™ Dinner
   Rolls, thawed but still cold
soft butter or squeeze margarine

Using 1 Texas roll (or 2 dinner rolls combined into a ball), make 4 or 5 deep cuts
into each roll with scissors, cutting nearly to the bottom. Brush butter or squeeze
margarine into each cut and place rolls in sprayed muffin cups.

Cover with sprayed plastic wrap. Let rise until double in size. Remove wrap and bake
at 350°F 15-20 minutes or until golden brown.

White-N-Wheat Braided Bread

1 Loaf Rhodes™ White Bread Dough,
  thawed but still cold
1 Loaf Rhodes™ 100% Wheat Bread Dough,
  thawed but still cold

Cut a loaf of white and a loaf of wheat in thirds lengthwise. Roll each third into a 12-inch rope. Braid one loaf with 2 white and 1 wheat rope and the other loaf with 2 wheat and 1 white. Place in a sprayed 4 1/2 x 8 1/2 - inch bread pan. Cover with sprayed plastic wrap and let rise until 1-inch above the pan. Remove wrap and bake at 350°F 25-30 minutes.

16

Cheddar Bread

1 Loaf Rhodes™ Frozen Bread Dough or 12
   Rhodes™ Dinner Rolls, thawed but still cold
1 egg beaten
1 cup grated sharp cheddar cheese
3 tablespoons dry ranch dressing mix
2 teaspoons parsley flakes, if desired

Cut dough into 1-inch pieces. In a medium sized bowl, toss dough pieces with egg. Add cheese, ranch dressing and parsley flakes and mix well. Place dough mixture on a cutting board and chop with a sharp knife into smaller pieces. Make sure mixture is well combined.

Place in a sprayed 4 1/2 x 8 1/2 -inch bread pan. Cover with plastic wrap and let rise to the top of the pan. Remove wrap and bake at 350°F 20-25 minutes or until golden brown.

Italian Herb Bread

12 Rhodes™ Dinner Rolls,
  thawed to room temperature
2 tablespoons butter, melted
1 tablespoon Parmesan cheese
½ teaspoon garlic salt with parsley
½ teaspoon oregano
½ teaspoon basil
1 tablespoon fresh chopped chives

Spray counter lightly with non-stick cooking spray. Combine rolls together and roll into a 10x14-inch rectangle. Place in a sprayed 9x13-inch baking pan. Cover with plastic wrap and let rise 30 minutes. Remove wrap and score dough, with a metal spatula or knife, into 2-inch squares.

In a small bowl, combine butter, Parmesan cheese, garlic salt, oregano and basil. Brush scored dough carefully with butter mixture and sprinkle with fresh chives. Replace wrap and let rise another 30 minutes. Remove wrap from dough and redefine score lines. Bake at 350°F 10-15 minutes or until golden brown.

Parmesan Cheese Knots

12 Rhodes Texas™ Rolls, thawed but still cold
1/2 cup grated Parmesan cheese
1 teaspoon dried parsley
1/2 teaspoon garlic salt
1/4 cup butter, melted

Roll each roll into a 9-inch rope. Tie in a knot. In a bowl, combine cheese, parsley and garlic salt. Dip each knot in melted butter and then in cheese mixture. Place in a sprayed 12-cup muffin tin. Cover with sprayed plastic wrap and let rise until double in size. Remove wrap and bake at 350°F 15-20 minutes or until golden brown.

Breakfast
&
Brunch

Start your day right with
these tasty and unique
recipes.

French Toast Pockets

1 Loaf Rhodes™ White Bread, baked, cooled, & sliced into 8 slices (day old)
8 ounces cream cheese, softened
2 teaspoons vanilla
6 tablespoons sugar, divided
1/2 cup coarsely chopped pecans
7 large eggs
1 cup milk
1/2 teaspoon nutmeg
1 cup crushed corn flakes
1/2 cup shredded coconut

Creamy Caramel Syrup
2 cups heavy cream
2 cups light Karo syrup
1 cup granulated sugar
1 cup light brown sugar, packed
1/8 teaspoon salt

Combine cream cheese, vanilla, chopped pecans and 2 tablespoons sugar. Set aside. Combine eggs, milk, nutmeg and 4 tablespoons sugar until well blended. Set aside. Combine crushed cornflakes with coconut and set aside. Cut down through the top and along one side of each slice of bread. Spread a generous tablespoon of cream cheese filling inside of each pocket. Preheat lightly greased electric griddle to 325°F. Dip bread pockets into egg/milk mixture, then into corn flake/coconut mixture. Coat both sides of each pocket slice. Cook until golden on both sides and each slice is warmed through. Serve warm with Creamy Caramel Syrup.

Creamy Caramel Syrup: Combine all ingredients in a saucepan. Stir over low heat until smooth. Bring to a rolling boil and maintain for 5 minutes. Continue to stir. Remove from heat and serve warm.

Mini Breakfast Pizzas

8 Rhodes™ Dinner Rolls,
   thawed to room temperature
8 eggs
salt & pepper to taste
1 tablespoon butter
4 tablespoons pizza sauce or salsa
½ cup grated cheddar cheese
½ cup grated mozzarella cheese
3 green onions, chopped
1 cup cubed, cooked ham
Italian seasoning, if desired

Spray counter lightly with non-stick cooking spray. Combine 2 rolls together and flatten into a 5-inch circle. Repeat with remaining rolls to make 4 mini pizza crusts. Place on a large sprayed baking sheet. Poke each one several times, with a fork, to prevent bubbles from forming. Bake at 350°F 10-15 minutes or until lightly browned. Remove from oven and set aside.

In a small bowl, whisk eggs. Melt butter in a skillet and add eggs. Cook and stir over medium heat until eggs are softly set. Salt & pepper to taste. Spread each mini pizza crust with 1 tablespoon pizza sauce or salsa. Combine the cheeses together and sprinkle each pizza with 1-2 tablespoons cheese. Top with eggs, green onions, ham and any remaining cheese. Sprinkle with Italian seasoning if desired. Bake at 375°F 10-15 minutes or until cheese is nicely melted.

Becca's Breakfast Sandwich

2 slices Rhodes™ White Bread, baked ahead
    following package instructions
1-2 strips bacon
2 sun dried tomatoes, packed in oil
1-2 eggs
1 teaspoon sour cream
salt and pepper
2 thin slices Gruyere cheese
butter

Slice bread and set aside. Cut bacon into
1/4-inch strips and fry in a small frying
pan on medium low. Cut the sun dried
tomatoes into 1/4-inch strips and place in
another pan on medium low. Allow to
heat for 1 minute then add eggs and sour
cream to the pan.

Season with salt & pepper and gently
scramble. Place one slice of cheese over
eggs. Begin toasting sliced bread. Drain
bacon strips on a paper towel. Butter
toast and place half of the bacon and the
eggs, cheese side down on one slice.

Top eggs with remaining bacon and
second slice of cheese. Place remaining
slice of toast on top.

Cinnamon Roll Ring

Rhodes™ Cinnamon Rolls
or 12 Rhodes Anytime!™ Cinnamon Rolls
am cheese frosting (included with rolls)

Place rolls on a sprayed 12-inch pizza pan or baking sheet. Cover with plastic wrap and let thaw for 1 hour. Remove wrap and arrange rolls in a 9-inch ring overlapping each other. (If using AnyTime! Cinnamon Rolls bake immediately at 350°F 15-20 minutes.) Cover with plastic wrap and let rise until double.

Remove wrap and bake at 350°F 20 minutes or until golden brown. Microwave frosting for 10 seconds and brush over warm rolls.

French Toast Sticks

1 Loaf Rhodes™ Frozen Bread Dough,
   baked according to package directions
3 eggs
1/4 cup milk
1/4 teaspoon salt
3/4 cup strawberry preserves
powdered sugar and cinnamon, if desired

Remove all crusts from baked bread and cut into 10 equal slices. Spread preserves on 5 slices of bread and top with remaining 5 slices. Cut each sandwich into 3 sticks. In a small bowl, combine eggs, milk and salt. Mix well.

Dip both sides of sticks in egg mixture. Cook on a sprayed medium hot griddle on each side until golden brown. Remove from griddle and sprinkle with powdered sugar and cinnamon if desired.

Farm Breakfast Casserole

1 Loaf Rhodes™ Bread Dough,
  baked and cooled
1 pound sliced bacon, diced
1 small yellow onion, chopped
2 ½ cups chopped fully cooked ham
1 ½ cups frozen southern
  style hash browns
3 cups shredded cheddar cheese
8 large eggs
3 cups milk
1 tablespoon Worcestershire sauce
1 teaspoon ground dry mustard
¼ teaspoon salt
¼ teaspoon pepper

Slice and cube baked bread. Set aside. In a skillet, cook bacon until crisp; add onion. Cook and stir until onion is tender; drain and add ham. In a sprayed 9x13-inch pan, layer half the bread cubes, potatoes and cheese. Top with all of the bacon mixture. Repeat layers of bread, potatoes and cheese. In a bowl, beat eggs; add milk, Worcestershire sauce, mustard, salt and pepper.

Pour egg mixture over bread layers. Cover and refrigerate overnight or at least 4 hours. Remove from refrigerator 30 minutes before baking. Remove covering and bake at 325°F 65-70 minutes or until a knife inserted near the center comes out clean. Cover with foil last 15-20 minutes of baking, if necessary, to prevent over browning.

Cinnamon Marble Loaf French Toast with Butter Syrup

12 Rhodes™ Dinner Rolls, thawed but still cold
1/4 cup sugar
1 teaspoon cinnamon
3 eggs
1/2 cup milk

Butter Syrup:
1 cup butter
2 cups sugar
1 cup buttermilk
1 teaspoon vanilla
1 teaspoon maple flavor
1/2 teaspoon baking soda

Cut each dinner roll in half. In a small bowl mix sugar and cinnamon. Roll each roll half in the sugar mixture and place in a sprayed 81/2 x 41/2-inch loaf pan. Cover with sprayed plastic wrap and let rise until even with the top of the pan. Remove wrap and bake at 350ºF 20-25 minutes. Remove from pan to cool. Slice to desired thickness. In a shallow bowl, mix eggs and milk together. Dip bread slices in egg mixture to coat both sides and cook in a frying pan or griddle.

For syrup: Bring butter, sugar and buttermilk to a boil, stirring constantly. Remove from heat and stir in vanilla, maple and baking soda (syrup will bubble when baking soda is added).

Zesty Sausage Bundt

18 Rhodes™ Dinner Rolls, thawed but still cold
½ cup butter or margarine, melted
¼ cup fresh thyme, finely chopped
¼ cup fresh rosemary, finely chopped
¼ cup fresh parsley, finely chopped
1 cup grated Parmesan cheese
1 pound Italian sausage, cooked, crumbled and drained

Flatten each roll into a 4-inch circle. Place butter in a shallow bowl. Combine herbs and cheese and place in another shallow bowl. Coat both sides of each dough circle with butter and then with cheese mixture. Arrange 6 dough circles evenly in a large sprayed bundt pan, to cover the bottom. Circles will overlap. Sprinkle half the cooked sausage over dough. Repeat with 6 more dough circles and the remaining sausage. Add last 6 dough circles to the top to cover sausage.

Cover with plastic wrap and let rise until almost double. Remove wrap and bake at 350°F 35-40 minutes. Cover with foil during last 10 minutes of baking. Remove from oven and invert onto serving platter.

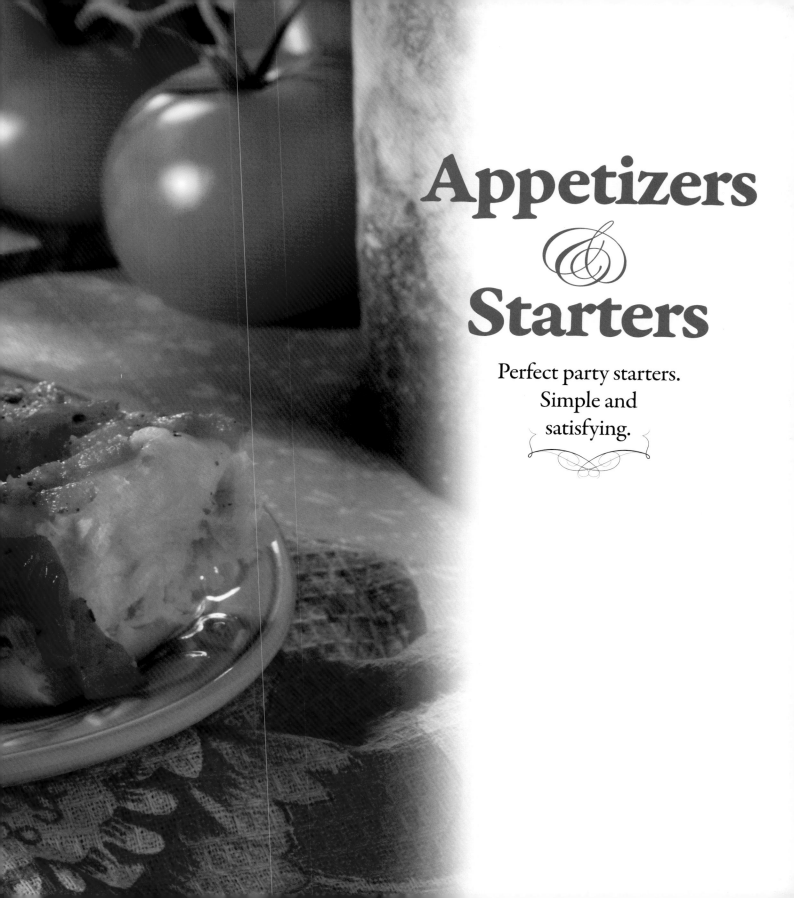

Appetizers & Starters

Perfect party starters.
Simple and
satisfying.

Chopped Jalapeno Cheese Bread

18 Rhodes™ Dinner Rolls,
  thawed to room temperature
1 1/2 cups grated sharp
  cheddar cheese
2 jalapeno peppers, seeded and
chopped
1/2 bunch cilantro, chopped
1 teaspoon garlic salt

Place rolls on a bread board. Top with
cheese, jalapenos & cilantro. Sprinkle
with garlic salt. Chop everything
together, with a knife and knead
with hands until ingredients are well
mixed into dough. Shape into a
large round loaf.

Place loaf on a large sprayed
baking sheet. Cover with sprayed
plastic wrap. Let rise until double.
Remove wrap and bake at 350°F
25-30 minutes.

Double Cheese Pinwheels

8 Rhodes™ Dinner Rolls,
thawed to room temperature
1 tablespoon butter, melted
1/4 cup grated Parmesan cheese
1/4 cup grated sharp cheddar cheese
1/2 teaspoon dill weed

Flatten each roll into a 4-inch square. Brush each one with melted butter and place on a large sprayed baking sheet. In a small bowl, combine cheeses and dill. Divide cheese mixture equally between the 8 squares and sprinkle over butter. Make diagonal cuts from each corner to within 1/2-inch of center. Fold alternating corners to center, overlapping slightly. Insert toothpick in center of each pinwheel to hold points down.

Cover with sprayed plastic wrap and let rise 30-45 minutes. Remove wrap and bake at 350°F 10-15 minutes or until golden brown. Remove toothpicks before serving.

45

Stuffed Pizza Pull-Aparts

22 Rhodes™ Dinner Rolls, thawed but still cold
44 small slices pepperoni
8 ounce brick mozzarella cheese, cut into 22 pieces
1/4 cup butter, melted
1 teaspoon dried basil
1 teaspoon dried oregano
1 teaspoon dried parsley
3/4 cup grated Parmesan cheese
pizza sauce

Spray counter lightly with non-stick cooking spray. Flatten each roll into a 3-inch circle. Place 2 pepperoni slices and 1 piece of mozzarella cheese on each circle. Pull edges of each dough circle up to completely enclose filling. In a small bowl combine butter, basil, oregano and parsley. Place Parmesan cheese in a separate bowl. Dip each filled roll in butter mixture and then in Parmesan cheese. Place 11 filled rolls in the bottom of a large sprayed bundt pan pinched sides up. Top with remaining 11 rolls. Sprinkle any remaining Parmesan cheese over rolls. Cover with plastic wrap and let rise until double. Remove wrap and bake at 350°F 30-35 minutes. Cover with foil last 10 minutes of baking if necessary to prevent over browning. Remove from oven and invert onto serving platter. Serve warm with heated pizza sauce.

Bleu Cheese Appetizer

12 Rhodes™ Dinner Rolls,
  thawed to room temperature
1 tablespoon olive oil
2 teaspoons dried basil
2 teaspoons dried oregano
1 teaspoon garlic powder
1 small red onion, thinly sliced
  and separated into rings
3 roma tomatoes, chopped
³/₄ cup crumbled bleu cheese
2 tablespoons grated Parmesan cheese

Spray counter lightly with non-stick cooking spray. Combine rolls together and roll into an 11x17-inch rectangle. Place on a sprayed 11x17-inch baking pan. Cover with sprayed plastic wrap and let rise 15-20 minutes. Remove wrap and poke with a fork several times to prevent bubbles from forming. Brush with oil and sprinkle with basil, oregano and garlic powder.

Bake at 350°F 10-15 minutes. Arrange onions and tomatoes over crust and sprinkle with cheeses. Bake at 350°F an additional 10 minutes.

Pizza Cups

12 Rhodes™ Dinner Rolls,
  thawed to room temperature
1 pound extra lean ground beef
1 1/2 cups pizza sauce
1 teaspoon Italian seasoning
salt & pepper to taste
3/4 cup grated mozzarella cheese, divided
fresh basil, if desired

Spray counter lightly with non-stick
cooking spray. Flatten each roll into a
5-inch circle. Cover with plastic wrap
and let rest. Brown ground beef in a
skillet. Stir in pizza sauce. Add Italian
seasoning and salt & pepper to taste.
Heat through. Remove wrap from
dough circles. Evenly press a circle into
each cup of a sprayed 12 cup muffin
tin to cover bottom and sides.

Divide 1/2 cup cheese evenly between
the 12 muffin cups and sprinkle over
dough in bottom of each cup. Divide
beef mixture evenly and spoon over
cheese. Bake at 350°F 20 minutes.
Remove from oven and divide
remaining cheese evenly between
cups and sprinkle over top of meat.
Bake an additional 5-10 minutes.

Green Chili Cheese Rolls

8 Rhodes Texas™ Rolls or 12 Rhodes™ Dinner
  Rolls, thawed to room temperature
1 tablespoon butter
2 cups chopped onion
8 ounce can chopped green chiles
2 cups grated sharp cheddar cheese

Spray board or counter with non-stick cooking spray. Combine rolls together and roll into a 13x15-inch rectangle. Melt butter in skillet and saute onions until soft and clear. Remove from heat and add green chiles.

Spread mixture over dough and sprinkle with cheese. Roll up lengthwise, jelly roll style. Slice dough into 12 equal pieces and place in a sprayed 9x13-inch pan. Cover with sprayed plastic wrap and let double in size. Remove wrap and bake at 350°F 20-25 minutes or until lightly browned.

Grilled Chicken Quesadillas

32 Rhodes™ Dinner Rolls or 16 Rhodes Texas™
  Rolls, thawed to room temperature
3 cups chopped cooked chicken, seasoned with
salt & lemon pepper
2 cups prepared salsa
2 cups grated sharp cheddar cheese
1 cup canned black beans, drained
1 cup canned whole kernel corn, drained
1/2 cup chopped cilantro
1/4 cup butter, melted

Spray counter lightly with non-stick spray. Roll two dinner rolls combined or 1 Texas roll into an 8-inch circle (dough will be thin). Place in a small sprayed skillet on the stove top and cook on each side 1-2 minutes or until very lightly browned. Repeat with remaining rolls to make 16 flatbread circles. In a large bowl combine chicken, salsa, cheese, beans, corn and cilantro. Brush melted butter over one side of each flatbread. Spread chicken mixture evenly over unbuttered side of 8 flatbreads. Top with remaining flatbreads, buttered side up. Grill at medium high heat on a sprayed grill or grill pan for about 3 minutes on each side or until cheese is melted and flatbread is browned.

Cheesy
Italian Bread

18 Rhodes™ Dinner Rolls,
  thawed but still cold
1 1/2 cups grated sharp cheddar cheese
1 yellow onion, finely chopped
1/4 cup olive oil
1 tablespoon Italian seasoning
1 teaspoon dried oregano
1 teaspoon dried basil

Cut each roll into fourths. Place
in a large bowl and toss with
cheese, onion, olive oil and spices
until well combined. Place in a
sprayed 9x9-inch square baking
pan. Cover with plastic wrap and
let rise until double. Remove
wrap and bake at 350°F 30-40
minutes. Cover with foil last 10
minutes, if needed, to prevent
over browning.

Basil Tomato Rolls

18 Rhodes™ Dinner Rolls,
  thawed to room temperature
5 tablespoons fresh, chopped basil
1 ½ cups shredded fresh Parmesan cheese
½ cup olive oil
2 teaspoons coarsely ground pepper, divided
4 medium tomatoes, chopped & seeded
¼ teaspoon sugar

Spray counter lightly with non-stick cooking spray. Combine rolls together and roll into a 12x18-inch rectangle. Cover with plastic wrap and let rest 10-15 minutes. Combine basil, cheese, oil, 1 teaspoon pepper and set aside. Place tomatoes in a colander to drain. Remove wrap from dough and spread evenly with basil mixture. Roll up jelly roll style and cut into 12 equal pieces. Combine drained tomatoes, remaining teaspoon pepper and sugar and arrange evenly in the bottom of a sprayed 9x13-inch baking pan. Top with basil filled rolls, cut side down. Cover with sprayed plastic wrap and allow to rise for about 1 hour. Remove wrap and bake on lower shelf at 350°F 25-30 minutes. Cover with foil last 5-10 minutes of baking if necessary to prevent over browning. Cool 5 minutes and invert onto a serving platter.

Wiggly Worm Sticks & Creeping Caterpillars

Rhodes™ Dinner Rolls, thawed but still cold
milk
Parmesan cheese
cinnamon/sugar
chocolate sprinkles

Wiggly Worm Sticks

Cut one dinner roll into 4 equal pieces. Roll each piece into a 5-6 inch worm. Place on a sprayed baking sheet. Snip some shallow lines across the top of the worm with the tip of your scissors. Bake at 350°F 10-15 minutes or until lightly browned. When cool, dip them into cheese dip or chocolate pudding topped with crushed chocolate cookies, if desired.

Creeping Caterpillars

Cut one roll into 8 equal pieces. Roll each piece into a ball. For cinnamon/sugar caterpillars dip each ball into milk and place on a sprayed baking sheet in the shape of a caterpillar. Sprinkle with the cinnamon/sugar mixture. For Parmesan caterpillars, dip each ball in milk and then dip in cheese and place on baking sheet. Bake at 350°F 10-15 minutes. When cooled, poke some holes for eyes with a toothpick. Place a chocolate sprinkle in each hole.

57

Pepperoni Swirls

1 Loaf Rhodes™ White or Wheat Bread,
   thawed to room temperature
6 ounces sliced pepperoni
1 small green pepper, thinly sliced
4 green onions, thinly sliced
sliced tomatoes, if desired
olives, if desired

Spray counter lightly with non-stick cooking spray. Divide the loaf in half. Roll each half into a 6x12-inch rectangle. Layer half of the pepperoni on each rectangle, lengthwise, leaving one inch along one long side bare. Brush the bare inch of dough with water. Evenly distribute the peppers and green onions over the pepperoni. Starting with the long edge opposite the bare edge, tightly roll up both rectangles and pinch edges to seal. Place both on a large sprayed baking sheet. Cover with sprayed plastic wrap and let rise 30 minutes. Remove wrap and bake at 350° F 20-25 minutes. Cool and then slice. Serve with sliced tomatoes and olives if desired.

Bread Sticks & Twists

Crunchy, crispy, savory and cheesy. Something for everyone.

Buttery Breadsticks

24 Rhodes™ Dinner Rolls, thawed but still cold
1/2 cup butter or margarine, melted
1/2 cup grated Parmesan cheese
garlic salt

Roll each roll into a 6-inch rope. Place butter and cheese in shallow bowls. Dip each rope into butter and then into Parmesan cheese. Place breadsticks on an 11x17-inch sprayed baking sheet in 2 rows of twelve each.

Sprinkle with garlic salt, if desired. Cover with plastic wrap. Let rise until double in size. Remove wrap and bake at 350°F 20 minutes or until golden brown.

Crisp Onion Breadsticks

18 Rhodes™ Dinner Rolls, thawed but still cold
2 eggs, beaten
1 teaspoon flour
1 teaspoon garlic salt
1/2 teaspoon dried parsley flakes
1 teaspoon dried rosemary
1/4 cup grated Parmesan cheese
3 cups French fried onions, crushed

Cut rolls in half. Roll each half into a 6-7 inch rope. Twist two ropes together and pinch both ends together. In a shallow bowl combine eggs, flour, salt, parsley flakes, rosemary and cheese. Place the onions in another shallow bowl. Dip each breadstick in the egg mixture, then roll in onions. Place 2-inches apart on large sprayed baking sheets. Cover with sprayed plastic wrap and let rise until double in size. Remove wrap and bake at 350°F 15-20 minutes.

Breadstick Blossoms

20 Rhodes™ Dinner Rolls,
  thawed but still cold (makes 8 blossoms)
2 tablespoons butter, melted
Parmesan cheese
garlic salt

Cut each dinner roll into 4 equal pieces. Each blossom takes 10 pieces. Roll one piece into a ball for the center of each blossom and place on a large sprayed baking sheet. Shape 5 pieces into petals, 2 combined together into a stem and 2 into leaves. Place around the center to form the blossom. Brush with butter and sprinkle lightly with Parmesan cheese and garlic salt. Repeat above steps with remaining roll pieces. Cover with plastic wrap and let rise 30-45 minutes. Remove wrap and bake at 350°F 15-20 minutes.

Crusty Garlic Twists

18 Rhodes™ Dinner Rolls,
   thawed to room temperature
1/4 cup olive oil
3 garlic cloves, minced
1/2 teaspoon salt
1/2 teaspoon pepper
1 cup grated fresh Parmesan cheese, divided
2 tablespoons finely chopped rosemary
1 tablespoon finely chopped thyme
additional olive oil, cheese and salt, if desired

Spray counter lightly with non-stick cooking spray. Combine 9 rolls together and roll into a 10x16-inch rectangle. Cover with plastic wrap and let rest. Repeat with remaining rolls to make two rectangles. In a small bowl combine olive oil, garlic, salt and pepper. In another bowl combine 1/2 cup cheese, rosemary and thyme. Remove wrap from dough and brush one rectangle with half of the olive oil mixture. Sprinkle cheese mixture over olive oil.

Place second rectangle over cheese mixture and press down lightly with hands. Cut, along the 16-inch side into 18 equal pieces (less than 1-inch wide). Twist each one several times and place on sprayed baking sheets. Brush with remaining olive oil mixture and sprinkle with remaining 1/2 cup cheese. Bake at 350°F 18-20 minutes or until golden brown and crusty. Remove from oven and brush with additional olive oil if desired. Sprinkle with additional cheese or salt, if desired.

Twisty Buttery Breadsticks

12 Rhodes™ Dinner Rolls, thawed but still cold
¼ cup butter, melted
¼ cup grated Parmesan cheese
garlic salt, if desired

Roll each roll into a 16-inch rope. Roll each end in opposite directions about 3 or 4 times. Pick up and pinch ends together. The breadstick will twist. Place butter and cheese in shallow bowls. Dip each breadstick in melted butter and then in Parmesan cheese.

Place on a sprayed baking sheet about 1-inch apart. Sprinkle with garlic salt, if desired. Cover with sprayed plastic wrap and let rise until double in size. Remove wrap and bake at 350°F 15-20 minutes or until golden brown.

Asiago Cheese Breadsticks

20 Rhodes Texas™ Rolls or 30 Rhodes™ Dinner Rolls,
   thawed to room temperature
1/2 cup butter melted
1-2 cups grated Asiago cheese
dried parsley, if desired

Stretch and roll each Texas roll or 1 1/2 dinner rolls combined into a 14-inch rope (rolls will relax and end up being about 11-inches long). Place butter in shallow bowl. Dip each rope in butter and place horizontally on an 11x17-inch jelly roll pan. Drizzle any remaining butter over rolls. Sprinkle cheese over top and then parsley, if desired.

Cover with plastic wrap and let rise until double in size, about 45-60 minutes. Remove wrap and bake at 350°F 20-25 minutes. Cover with foil last 5-10 minutes of baking if necessary to prevent cheese from over browning. Serve warm.

Cheesy Potato Chip Breadsticks

12 Rhodes Texas™ Rolls or 24 Rhodes™ Dinner
   Rolls, thawed but still cold
12 strips pepper jack cheese
1/4 cup butter or margarine, melted
3/4 cup crushed sour cream and onion potato
chips

Roll each Texas™ roll or 2 dinner rolls combined into a 7-inch rope. Flatten each rope. Cut twelve 6-inch strips of cheese 1/2- inch thick. Place one strip of cheese on each flattened rope. Tightly pinch dough around cheese to form a breadstick.

Place butter and potato chips in shallow bowls. Roll each breadstick in butter and then in crushed potato chips. Place seam side up on a sprayed baking sheet. Cover with plastic wrap and let rise until double. Remove wrap and bake at 350°F 20 minutes or until golden brown.

Dutch Oven Buttery Breadsticks

4 Rhodes™ Dinner Rolls, thawed but still cold
⅓ cup butter, melted
½ cup Parmesan cheese
arlic salt

Pour melted butter into a 12-inch Dutch oven. Roll each roll into a 7-inch rope. Roll each rope in butter in the Dutch oven until completely coated. Place cheese in a bowl and roll buttered breadsticks in cheese. Return breadsticks to dutch oven and coil end to end starting on the outside edge. Cover with lid and let rise until double. Bake at 350°F 15-20 minutes.

Dutch Oven Temperature Control using Briquets:
350°F in a 12-inch Dutch oven, oven top 16, oven bottom 8

Pizzas & Calzones

Think outside the box.
Home-baked
fresh from your
oven.

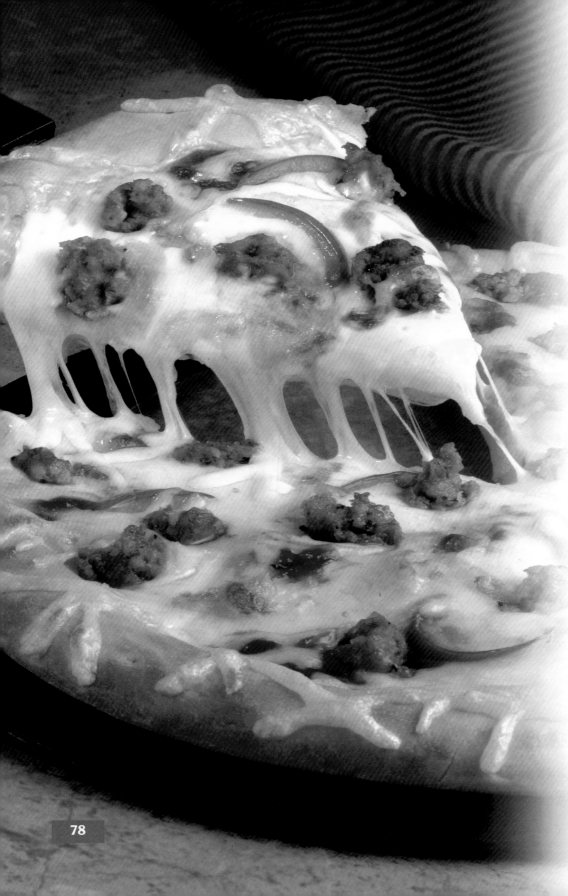

Easy Homemade Pizza

Rhodes
Classic
Recipe

10 Rhodes™ Dinner Rolls,
  thawed to room temperature
1/2 cup pizza sauce
2 cups grated mozzarella cheese
Suggested toppings: sausage (cooked),
pepperoni, onions, mushrooms, olives,
green peppers, tomatoes

Spray counter lightly
with non-stick cook-
ing spray. Combine
rolls together and
roll into a 13-inch
circle and place on
a slightly smaller
12-inch sprayed
pizza pan (dough
will spring back a
little as it rests).

Cover with sprayed
plastic wrap and
let rise 30 minutes.

Remove plastic
wrap and spread
sauce over crust.
Add desired
toppings and
sprinkle with cheese.

Bake at 425°F 15 minutes
or until crust is golden.

Bubbly Bread

Rhodes Classic Recipe

5 Rhodes Texas™ Rolls or 10 Rhodes™ Dinner
  Rolls, thawed to room temperature
1/3 cup grated Parmesan cheese
3/4 cup grated mozzarella cheese
seasoned salt and fresh ground black pepper

Sprinkle bread board with Parmesan cheese. Combine rolls together. Place on top of cheese and begin rolling out into a 14-inch circle. Turn dough over a few times as you continue to roll the cheese into the dough. Place on a sprayed 12-inch pizza pan. Sprinkle with mozzarella cheese, seasoned salt and fresh ground black pepper.

Cover with sprayed plastic wrap. Let rise 30 minutes. Remove wrap and bake at 350°F 15-20 minutes. Serve warm, or store up to 2 days. Consider using the crust to make a quick pizza.

Thai Peanut Pizza

9 Rhodes™ Dinner Rolls or 6 Rhodes
 Texas™ Rolls, thawed to room temperature
2 boneless skinless chicken breasts, cubed
1 tablespoon canola oil
1 tablespoon low sodium soy sauce
1 red bell pepper, cut into strips
3 green onions, chopped
2 cups grated mozzarella cheese
1 cucumber, sliced
1/2 cup chopped cilantro

peanut sauce:
1/4 cup sugar
1/4 cup creamy peanut butter
3 tablespoons low sodium soy sauce
3 tablespoons water
2 tablespoons canola oil
2 teaspoons minced garlic

Spray counter lightly with non-stick cooking spray. Combine Texas™ rolls or dinner rolls together and roll into a 13-inch circle. Place on a sprayed 12-inch pizza pan. Cover with sprayed plastic wrap and let rise 30 minutes.

Remove wrap and poke several times with a fork to prevent bubbles from forming. Bake at 350°F 10-15 minutes or until lightly browned. In a medium saucepan, combine all the ingredients for the peanut sauce. Cook over medium-low heat, stirring constantly, 10-15 minutes or until thickened. Set aside to cool. Stir fry the chicken in canola oil and soy sauce until completely cooked. Spread peanut sauce over baked crust (peanut sauce can be made ahead and stored in the refrigerator). Top with red peppers, green onions, cooked chicken and cheese.

Bake at 350°F 10-15 minutes or until cheese is melted. Remove from oven and top with cucumbers and cilantro.

Red Potato Focaccia

12 Rhodes™ Dinner Rolls or 8 Rhodes
 Texas™ Rolls, thawed to room temperature
5 medium size red potatoes,
 washed & thinly sliced
2 teaspoons rosemary
4 tablespoons olive oil, divided
1/2 teaspoon garlic salt
salt & fresh ground black pepper to taste

Spray counter lightly with non-stick
cooking spray. Combine rolls together
and roll into a 14-inch circle or
11x17-inch rectangle. Cover dough
with plastic wrap and let rest.

Mix potatoes, rosemary and 2
tablespoons olive oil in a microwave
safe dish. Microwave for 3 minutes on
high. Stir, rotate and cook for an
additional 3 minutes. Remove wrap
from dough and place on a sprayed
14-inch pizza pan or 11x17-inch
baking sheet. Cover with plastic wrap
and let rise for 30 minutes.

Remove wrap and press dough
down with fingers to form a dimpled
surface. Combine remaining 2
tablespoons olive oil with garlic
salt and brush over dough. Spread
potatoes evenly over dough. Sprinkle
with salt and fresh ground pepper.
Bake at 350°F 25-30 minutes.

81

Smiley Face Pizza

2 Rhodes™ Dinner Rolls,
  thawed to room temperature
favorite pizza toppings

Combine rolls together and flatten into a 6-inch circle. Place on sprayed baking sheet. Poke several times with a fork to prevent bubbles from forming. Bake at 350°F 10-12 minutes. Remove from oven and let cool slightly.

Spread with sauce. Top with grated cheese. Bake at 350°F 8-10 minutes or until cheese is nicely melted. Remove from oven and make face using sliced mozzarella rounds with olives for eyes, pepperoni for nose and eyebrows and a green pepper slice for mouth.

Garden Pockets

3 Rhodes™ Dinner Rolls, thawed but still cold
ounces fresh mushrooms, sliced
bunch green onions including tops, chopped
tablespoons olive oil
roma tomatoes, chopped
medium green pepper, sliced
cup pizza sauce
teaspoons fresh oregano
lt & pepper to taste
cup grated mozzarella cheese
cup grated Parmesan cheese
egg, beaten
ditional Parmesan cheese and garlic salt, if desired

Press 3 rolls together and, using a little flour, roll them into a 7-inch circle. Make 5 more circles with the other rolls. Cover with sprayed plastic wrap and set aside. In a large skillet, saute mushrooms and onion in oil for 1-2 minutes. Add tomatoes and green pepper and toss together. Stir in pizza sauce. In a small bowl combine cheeses together. Remove wrap from rolls. Divide filling equally and spoon onto one half of each circle. Divide cheese equally and place on top of filling. Brush edges of dough with water. Fold each circle in half and press edges with a fork to seal.

Place on a large sprayed baking sheet. Brush with beaten egg and sprinkle with Parmesan cheese and garlic salt, if desired. Bake at 350°F 20-25 minutes or until golden brown.

Buffalo Chicken Pizza

8 Rhodes™ Dinner Rolls,
  thawed to room temperature
2-6 ounce boneless chicken breasts, diced
1 tablespoon olive oil
smoked paprika
cayenne pepper
2 tablespoons butter, melted
½ cup Franks Red Hot Sauce
¼ cup bleu cheese dressing
1 cup grated mozzarella cheese
celery, for garnish

Spray counter lightly with non-stick cooking spray. Flatten each roll into a 5-inch circle. Cover with plastic wrap and let rest. Lightly spray frying pan with non-stick cooking spray. Cook diced chicken in olive oil and season with smoked paprika and cayenne pepper. Remove from heat. In a small bowl, combine butter and hot sauce and pour over chicken to evenly coat.

Remove wrap from dough circles and place circles on a sprayed baking sheet. Top with bleu cheese dressing. Arrange chicken evenly over dressing. Sprinkle with mozzarella cheese. Bake at 400°F 10-15 minutes. Remove from oven and garnish with celery.

Calzones or Pizza Pockets

12 Rhodes Texas™ Rolls, thawed but still cold
flour
2 ounces sliced pepperoni
8 ounces sausage, browned and drained well
4 1/2 ounce can sliced olives, drained
1/2 cup sliced fresh mushrooms
1/2 cup chopped green pepper
1 cup grated mozzarella cheese
1 teaspoon Italian seasoning
1 cup pizza sauce, heated

Press 3 rolls together and, using a little flour, roll them into a 12-inch circle. Make three more circles with the other rolls. Combine pepperoni, sausage, olives, mushrooms, green peppers, cheese and Italian seasoning. Divide mixture equally and spoon onto one half of each circle. Fold dough over (like a turnover) and pinch edges together to seal.

Place on a large sprayed baking sheet. Bake at 350°F 20-25 minutes or until golden brown. To serve, dip in heated pizza sauce.

Tuscan Tomato Tart

9 Rhodes™ Dinner Rolls or 6 Rhodes Texas™
  Rolls, thawed to room temperature
1 tablespoon olive oil
2 tablespoons prepared pesto
2 tablespoons Italian flavored bread crumbs
1 cup crumbled feta cheese, divided
1 tablespoon fresh chopped oregano
1 tomato, cut into ¼-inch slices
1 yellow or orange tomato,
  cut into ¼-inch slices
6-7 fresh basil leaves, thinly sliced

Spray counter lightly with non-stick cooking spray. Combine dinner or Texas rolls together and roll into a 13-inch circle. Place on a sprayed 12-inch pizza pan. Cover with sprayed plastic wrap and let rise 20-30 minutes. Remove wrap and poke with a fork several times. Bake at 350°F 10-15 minutes.

Remove from oven and let cool slightly. Brush with olive oil and spread with pesto. Sprinkle with bread crumbs and ½ cup feta cheese. Sprinkle oregano over cheese. Top with tomatoes. Sprinkle with remaining cheese and basil. Bake for an additional 10-15 minutes.

Cheese Stuffed Focaccia

Rhodes™ Dinner Rolls or 16 Rhodes Texas™
Rolls, thawed to room temperature
tablespoons olive oil, divided
slices Provolone cheese
/2 cups grated Jarlsburg cheese
ablespoons chopped fresh basil, divided
ablespoon chopped fresh oregano
ablespoon chopped fresh thyme
ablespoon chopped fresh rosemary
loves garlic, minced
cup grated fresh Parmesan cheese

Spray counter lightly with non-stick cooking spray. Combine 12 rolls together and roll into a 10x15-inch rectangle. Cover with plastic wrap and let rest 10 minutes. Repeat above step with remaining 12 rolls. Remove wrap and place one dough rectangle on a sprayed 10x15-inch baking pan. Brush with 1 tablespoon olive oil. Cover with Provolone and Jarlsburg cheeses and sprinkle with 3 tablespoons basil, the oregano, thyme, rosemary and garlic. Top with remaining dough rectangle. Pinch bottom and top layers of dough together to seal. Brush with remaining olive oil and sprinkle with Parmesan cheese and 1 tablespoon basil. Bake at 350°F 25-30 minutes. Slice and serve while warm.

Chicken Fajita Pizza

16 Rhodes™ Dinner Rolls or 10 Rhodes Texas™ Rolls, thawed to room temperature
1 pound boneless, skinless chicken, cut into 1-inch pieces
1 tablespoon olive oil
1 green pepper, sliced
1 cup thinly sliced onion
2 cloves garlic minced
2 teaspoons chili powder
1 teaspoon hot sauce
½ teaspoon salt
¾ cup salsa
1 ½ cups grated Monterey Jack or mozzarella cheese

Spray counter lightly with non-stick cooking spray. Combine dinner rolls or Texas rolls together and roll into a 15x10-inch rectangle. Place dough on a sprayed 15x10-inch baking pan. Cover with plastic wrap and let rise 20-30 minutes. Remove wrap and poke several times with a fork to prevent bubbles from forming. Bake at 375°F 10-15 minutes or until lightly browned. Remove from oven and set aside.

In a skillet, saute chicken in olive oil for about 5 minutes. Add the green pepper, onion, garlic, chili powder, hot sauce and salt. Cook 1-2 minutes longer. Spoon mixture over crust and top with salsa and cheese. Bake at 350°F 10-15 minutes or until crust is golden brown and cheese is melted. Serve with sour cream and/or guacamole, if desired.

Broccoli & Tomato Focaccia

Loaf Rhodes™ White Bread or 12 Dinner
Rolls, thawed to room temperature.
tablespoons olive oil, divided
teaspoon garlic salt
/2 cups mozzarella cheese, grated
cups broccoli florets, microwaved for 1 minute
cherry tomatoes, cut in half
cup fresh sliced mushrooms
small can sliced olives
t & pepper to taste

Spray counter lightly with non-stick cooking spray. Roll loaf or combined rolls into a
10x14-inch rectangle. Place in a 9x13-inch sprayed pan. Cover with plastic wrap and
let rise for 30 minutes.

Remove wrap. Press dough down with fingers to form a dimpled surface. Brush
with 1 tablespoon olive oil and sprinkle with garlic salt. Sprinkle mozzarella cheese,
broccoli, tomato, mushrooms and olives over the dough. Brush toppings with
remaining olive oil. Top with salt and pepper. Bake at 350°F 20-30 minutes.

Cheesy Pesto Bread

9 Rhodes™ Dinner rolls or 6 Rhodes Texas™
  rolls, thawed to room temperature
1 tablespoon butter, melted
1 teaspoon Italian seasoning
4 tablespoons prepared pesto
1 cup grated mozzarella cheese
½ cup shredded fresh Parmesan cheese

Spray counter lightly with non-stick cooking spray. Combine Texas™ or dinner rolls together and roll into a 13-inch circle. Place on a sprayed 12-inch pizza pan. Brush with butter and sprinkle with Italian seasoning.

Cover with plastic wrap and let rise 20-30 minutes. Remove wrap and poke several times with a fork to prevent bubbles from forming. Pre-bake at 350°F 10-12 minutes. Remove from oven and let cool slightly. Spread with pesto. Sprinkle cheeses over pesto. Bake at 350°F an additional 10-12 minutes or until cheese is melted.

Whole Wheat Vegetable Pizza

1 Loaf Rhodes™ Whole Wheat Bread Dough
or 8 Rhodes Whole Wheat Texas™ Rolls,
thawed to room temperature
(makes two 12-inch pizzas)
2 1/2 cups small broccoli florets
1 1/2 cups sliced yellow pepper
1/4 cup water
4 tablespoons pesto
2 cups grated provolone cheese
red onion sliced in thin rings
2 cloves garlic minced
salt and pepper if desired

Spray counter lightly with non-stick
cooking spray. Cut loaf in half or
combine 4 Texas rolls together and
roll into a 13-inch circle. Place on a
sprayed 12-inch pizza pan. Repeat
with remaining half loaf or 4 Texas
rolls. Poke each crust several times
with a fork to prevent bubbles from
forming. Bake at 350°F 8-10 minutes.
Remove from oven and set aside to
cool. Place broccoli and yellow pepper
in a bowl with water. Cover and
microwave 1-2 minutes until crisp-
tender. Remove from microwave and
drain.

Spread each partially baked crust with
2 tablespoons pesto. Sprinkle each
with 1/2 of the cheese and top with
broccoli, pepper & onion rings.
Sprinkle 1/2 of the minced garlic over
each pizza. Season with salt & pepper
if desired. Bake at 350°F an additional
9 minutes or until cheese is melted
and crusts are golden brown.

Black Bean & Corn Calzones

24 Rhodes™ Dinner Rolls,
  thawed to room temperature
1 ½ cups chopped yellow onion
½ cup diced sweet red pepper
½ cup diced green bell pepper
1 tablespoon olive oil
2 cloves garlic minced
1 ½ cups frozen corn, thawed and drained
14 ounces black beans, well drained
½ cup fresh salsa
1 teaspoon garlic salt
½ teaspoon pepper
1 ½ cups grated cheddar cheese
additional fresh salsa, if desired

Spray counter with non-stick cooking spray. Combine 2 rolls together and flatten into a 7-inch circle. Repeat with remaining rolls. Cover circles with plastic wrap and let rest. Saute onions and peppers in olive oil for 1 minute. Add garlic and continue cooking until onions are clear, about 3-4 minutes. Remove from heat and add corn, beans, salsa, salt and pepper. Remove wrap from dough circles and divide filling equally between circles. Divide cheese equally and sprinkle on top of filling. Moisten edges of dough circles with water. Fold dough over filling and press edges together with a fork.

Place on large sprayed baking sheets. With a sharp knife, cut vents in each calzone. Bake at 350°F 20-25 minutes. Serve with additional fresh salsa if desired.

Pork & Pineapple Pizza

12 Rhodes™ Dinner Rolls or 8 Rhodes Texas™
  Rolls, thawed to room temperature
8 ounce can pineapple tidbits, drained
  and juice reserved
2 tablespoons butter
1 teaspoon sugar
1/2 medium yellow onion
18 ounces ready to eat pulled barbecue pork
8 ounces grated mozzarella cheese

Spray counter lightly with non-stick cooking spray. Combine dinner rolls or Texas rolls together and roll into an 11x17-inch rectangle. Place on a sprayed 11x17-inch baking pan, building up edges slightly. Poke several times with a fork and pre-bake at 350°F 10-15 minutes. Remove from oven to cool.

In a small skillet, bring juice drained from pineapple to a low boil. Boil until reduced to about 2 tablespoons. Melt the butter into the juice. Add the sugar and stir until dissolved. Slice the onion into thin slices. Add to the pineapple mixture and saute, stirring frequently, until the onions begin to turn golden. Remove from heat and set aside. Spread the prebaked crust with pork. Sprinkle evenly with cheese, sauted onions and pineapple. Bake at 350°F 15-20 minutes or until cheese is nicely melted.

Personal Cheeseburger Pizza

16 Rhodes™ Dinner Rolls,
  thawed to room temperature
1/2 cup ketchup
2 tablespoons prepared mustard
3/4 pound lean ground beef
salt & pepper to taste
1 small sweet onion, thinly sliced
1 cup grated cheddar cheese
1 cup shredded lettuce
1 medium tomato, sliced and quartered
1/2 cup dill pickle slices

Spray counter lightly with non-stick cooking spray. Combine 4 rolls together and roll them into an 8-inch circle. Repeat for remaining rolls. Place on large sprayed baking sheets. Poke several times with a fork to prevent bubbles from forming . Bake at 350° 10-12 minutes or until lightly browned. Remove from oven and set aside.

Combine ketchup and mustard and divide evenly between circles. Spread to within 1-inch of edge. Brown ground beef and drain well. Salt and pepper to taste. Divide evenly between circles and sprinkle over sauce. Top with onions and grated cheese.

Bake at 350°F 15 minutes or until cheese is completely melted. Remove from oven and top with lettuce, tomatoes and pickles.

Corned Beef & Potato Pizza

16 Rhodes™ Dinner Rolls, or 10 Rhodes Texas™
 Rolls, thawed to room temperature
2 medium size yellow onions, thinly sliced
1 tablespoon olive oil
1 tablespoon fresh thyme leaves
2 medium size red potatoes, thinly sliced
1/2-1 teaspoon salt
1 teaspoon ground black pepper
2 cups grated Swiss cheese
4 - 6 ounces fully cooked corned beef,
 cut in strips
2 tablespoons grated Parmesan cheese

Spray counter lightly with non-stick cooking spray. Combine rolls together and roll into a 15-inch circle. Place on a sprayed 14-inch pizza pan. Turn up edge and pinch to form a rim. Cover with plastic wrap and let rise while preparing toppings. In a large skillet, cook onions in olive oil over medium heat 4 to 6 minutes or until soft. Reduce heat to low. Sprinkle thyme over onions and add potatoes. Cover and cook 8 to 10 minutes or until potatoes are tender. Remove from heat and season with salt & pepper.

Remove wrap from dough and poke several times with a fork to prevent bubbles from forming. Pre-bake crust at 350°F 10-15 minutes. Remove from oven and sprinkle with 1/2 of the Swiss cheese. Top with potato mixture. Return to oven and bake 10-15 minutes. Remove from oven and top with corned beef, remaining Swiss cheese and Parmesan cheese. Bake an additional 5-10 minutes or until cheese is melted.

Stuffed Crust Pizza

12 Rhodes™ Dinner Rolls or 1 Loaf
Rhodes™ Bread Dough, thawed to
　　room temperature
5 sticks mozzarella string cheese
½ cup pizza sauce
favorite pizza toppings

Spray counter lightly
with non-stick
cooking spray. Roll
combined rolls or
loaf into a 16-inch
circle. Cover with
plastic wrap and let
rest 10-15 minutes.

Remove wrap and
place on a 14-inch
sprayed pizza pan
(edges will overlap
pan). Cut each
string cheese in half
and arrange, 1-inch
in around the edge
of the dough circle.
Bring the edge of
the dough over the
cheese and press to seal it inside.
Continue this around the entire circle
Press seams a second time to make
sure they are fully sealed.

Top with sauce and your favorite
pizza toppings. Bake at 400°F
10-20 minutes or until crust is
golden brown.

Walnut Gorgonzola Pizza

9 Rhodes™ Dinner Rolls or 6 Rhodes Texas™
   Rolls, thawed to room temperature
2 tablespoons olive oil, divided
1 teaspoon sugar
2 or 3 medium red onions sliced
salt & pepper to taste
1 cup crumbled Gorgonzola cheese
1 cup walnut pieces

Spray counter lightly with non-stick cooking spray. Combine rolls together and roll into a 13-inch circle and place on a 12-inch sprayed pizza pan. Cover with plastic wrap and set aside. Heat 1 tablespoon olive oil in a skillet. Sprinkle with sugar, add onions and cook slowly, stirring frequently, about 20 minutes or until golden brown. Season with salt and pepper.

Remove wrap and spread onions over prepared pizza dough. Spread little chunks of Gorgonzola over the onions, then sprinkle with walnuts. Brush edge of crust lightly with remaining olive oil. Bake at 425°F for 12 minutes or until crust is golden and walnuts are toasty.

Red Onion Focaccia

12 Rhodes™ Dinner Rolls or 6 Texas™ Rolls
  or 1 Loaf Rhodes™ Bread Dough,
  thawed to room temperature
1 tablespoon olive oil
1 cup grated mozzarella cheese
½ cup plus 2 tablespoons grated Parmesan
  cheese, divided
½ red onion, thinly sliced
1 tablespoon Italian seasoning

Spray counter lightly with non-stick
cooking spray. Roll loaf or combined
rolls into a 13-inch circle.

Place dough on a sprayed 12-inch pizza
pan. Cover with plastic wrap and let
rest 10-15 minutes. Remove wrap and
poke dough several times with a fork.

Brush with olive oil and sprinkle
with mozzarella cheese and ½ cup
Parmesan cheese.

Arrange sliced onions over cheeses and
sprinkle with Italian seasoning. Top
with 2 tablespoons Parmesan cheese.
Bake at 400°F 12-15 minutes.

Italian Deep Dish Pizza

8 Rhodes™ Dinner Rolls or 12 Rhodes Texas™
 Rolls, thawed to room temperature
1/4 cup extra virgin olive oil
Italian seasoning
8 ounce can tomato sauce
1/2 cup crumbled feta cheese
4 cups grated mozzarella cheese
your choice of toppings, pepperoni, sausage,
olives etc.
1 cup grated cheddar cheese

Spray counter lightly with non-stick cooking spray. Combine rolls together and roll into a 13x18-inch rectangle. Pour olive oil in the bottom of a 12x17-inch baking pan. Rotate the pan so the olive oil coats the pan evenly. Sprinkle with Italian seasoning. Place dough in pan. Cover with sprayed plastic wrap and let rise for about an hour. As dough rises, you will need to press it out to the corners of the pan. Remove wrap and poke crust several times with a fork to prevent bubbles from forming. Pre-bake crust at 350°F 12 minutes.

Remove from oven and spread tomato sauce evenly over crust. Sprinkle sauce with Italian seasoning. Sprinkle evenly with feta cheese. Sprinkle mozzarella evenly over top of feta. Add your favorite toppings. Sprinkle cheddar cheese evenly over toppings. Bake at 425°F 12-15 minutes.

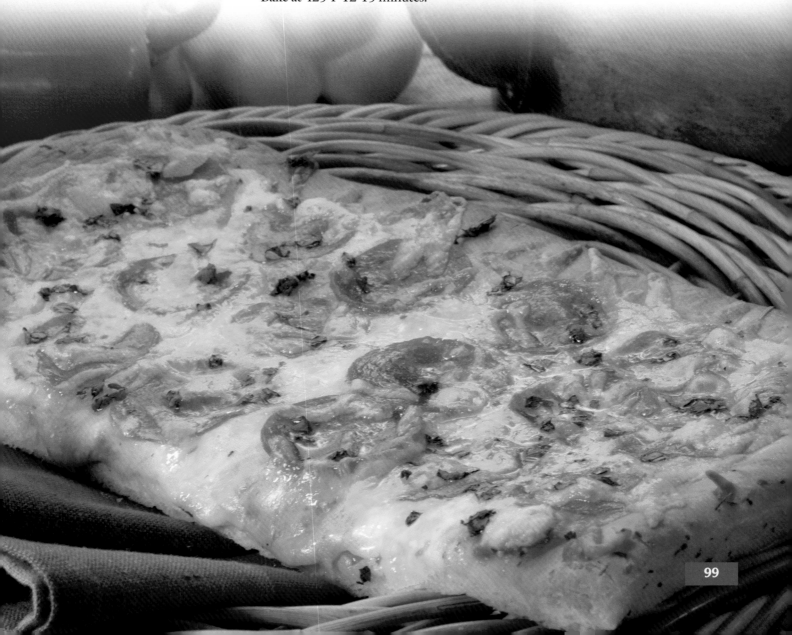

Cilantro Pesto Pizza

10 Rhodes™ Dinner Rolls,
  thawed to room temperature
1 pound boneless, skinless chicken breast,
  cut into 1-inch pieces
1 tablespoon taco seasoning
2 tablespoons olive oil
1 1/2 cups grated colby-Jack cheese
1/2 cup chopped tomatoes
2 tablespoons chopped green onion

Cilantro Pesto:
2 cups cilantro leaves
1 jalapeno pepper, seeded and chopped
2 cloves garlic, minced
3 tablespoons pine nuts or walnuts
2 tablespoons olive oil
1 tablespoon fresh lime juice
salt and pepper to taste

Spray counter lightly with non-stick cooking spray. Combine rolls together and roll into a 13-inch circle. Place on a slightly smaller 12-inch sprayed pizza pan (dough will spring back a little as it rests). Poke several times with a fork to prevent bubbles from forming. Bake at 350°F 10 minutes. Remove from oven to cool.

Combine cilantro pesto ingredients in a small food processor bowl and process until almost smooth. Spread evenly over cooled crust. In a bowl, combine chicken and taco seasoning and mix well. Heat olive oil in a skillet over medium heat. Add chicken and cook until cooked through. Place chicken evenly over pesto. Top with cheese, tomatoes and green onion. Bake at 350°F 10-15 minutes.

Grilled BBQ Chicken Pizza

Rhodes™ Dinner Rolls or 6 Rhodes Texas™
Rolls, thawed to room temperature
ounce boneless, skinless chicken breast,
ubed (or use barbecued chicken cubed)
cup barbecue sauce, divided
2 small green pepper, cut in thin strips
2 small red pepper, cut in thin strips
2 cup sliced mushrooms
small tomato, diced
cup grated mozzarella cheese

Cook chicken in $1/2$ cup barbecue sauce until no longer pink. Set aside. Spray counter lightly with non-stick cooking spray. Combine rolls together and roll into a 13-inch circle. Place on a sprayed 12-inch pizza pan. Build up edges slightly. Poke crust several times with a fork to prevent bubbles from forming.

Grill, covered, over medium heat for 10-15 minutes. Remove from grill. Spread with remaining $1/2$ cup barbecue sauce. Top with chicken mixture, peppers, mushrooms and tomato. Sprinkle with cheese. Grill, covered, 5-10 minutes longer, or until crust is golden and cheese is melted.

Stuffed Meatball Pizza

18 Rhodes™ Dinner Rolls or 12 Rhodes Texas™
   Rolls, thawed to room temperature
1 egg, beaten
2 cups grated Italian blend cheese, divided
16 ounce package pre-cooked, frozen, bite-
sized Italian meatballs
1 cup marinara sauce
1 teaspoon basil leaves
1 teaspoon crushed red pepper
Parmesan cheese
extra marinara sauce, for dipping

Spray counter lightly with non-stick cooking spray. Combine 9 dinner rolls or 6 Texas rolls together and roll into a 13-inch circle for bottom crust. Cover with plastic wrap and let rest. Repeat above steps with remaining rolls to make the top crust.

Remove wrap from first dough circle and place the dough in a sprayed 12-inch deep dish pizza pan to cover the bottom and 1/2-inch up the sides. Brush with beaten egg. Sprinkle with 1 cup grated Italian blend cheese. Top with frozen meatballs. Drizzle mariana sauce over meatballs and sprinkle with remaining grated cheese. Sprinkle with basil and crushed red pepper. Remove wrap from remaining dough circle and place dough over all ingredients. Press edges of bottom and top crusts together to seal

Brush top crust with beaten egg. Sprinkle with Parmesan cheese. Using a sharp knife, cut 2 vent holes in top crust. Bake at 350°F 35-40 minutes. Serve with extra marinara sauce for dipping.

Bacon Herb Focaccia

Loaf Rhodes™ Bread Dough or 12 Rhodes™
Dinner Rolls, thawed to room temperature
tablespoons olive oil
tablespoons grated Parmesan cheese
5 slices fully cooked bacon,
   cut into 1-inch pieces
tablespoons fresh rosemary, chopped

Spray counter lightly with non-stick cooking spray. Roll loaf or combined dinner rolls into a 10x14-inch rectangle. Place in a sprayed 9x13-inch baking pan. Brush with olive oil and sprinkle with cheese, bacon and rosemary. Cover with plastic wrap and let rise 30-45 minutes. Remove wrap and bake at 350°F 15-20 minutes or until golden brown.

Main Dishes
& Entrées

Inspiring new recipes that are sure to be a hit for dinner tonight.

Baked Reuben Braid

1 Loaf Rhodes™ Bread Dough or 12 Rhodes™
   Dinner Rolls, thawed to room temperature
1/3 cup light Italian cheese salad dressing
1/2 pound thinly sliced turkey pastrami
8 slices Swiss cheese
2 cups sauerkraut, drained
1 egg white, beaten
2 tablespoons caraway seeds

Spray counter lightly with non-stick cooking spray. Roll loaf or combined dinner rolls into a 12x16-inch rectangle. Cover with plastic wrap and let rest 10-15 minutes. Remove wrap from dough and make cuts 4-inches long and 1 1/2-inches apart on long sides of dough. Pour dressing lengthwise in a 4-inch strip down center of dough. Top with pastrami, Swiss cheese and sauerkraut.

Begin braid by folding top and bottom strips toward filling. Then braid strips left over right, right over left. Finish by pulling last strip over and tucking under braid.

Lift braid with both hands and place on a large sprayed baking sheet. Brush with egg white and sprinkle with caraway seeds. Bake at 350°F 30-35 minutes or until golden brown. Cool slightly and slice to serve.

Hot Diggity Dogs

Rhodes™ Dinner Rolls,
thawed to room temperature
bun length beef franks
cup grated cheddar cheese
ketchup, if desired

Combine two rolls together and flatten into a 7-inch oval. Repeat with remaining rolls to make 8 ovals. Place one frank in middle of each dough oval. Pull dough up around each frank to completely enclose. Pinch edges together to seal. Turn seam side down and place on large sprayed baking sheets. With a sharp knife, cut each one into 8 equal pieces, through top layer of dough and frank, leaving bottom layer of dough intact. Twist first cut piece to the left and second to the right. Repeat this for the rest of the pieces. Bake at 350°F 10 minutes. Remove from oven and sprinkle each one with 2 tablespoons grated cheese. Return to oven and bake an additional 5-10 minutes. Serve drizzled with ketchup, if desired.

107

Spinach Braid

1 Loaf Rhodes™ Bread Dough or 12 Rhodes™ Dinner
  Rolls, thawed to room temperature
8 ounces cream cheese, softened
3 cups chopped fresh spinach
1/2 teaspoon basil
1/2 teaspoon rosemary
1 egg
1/2 cup Parmesan cheese
2 cups chopped ham
1 cup sliced fresh mushrooms
1/2 cup chopped onion
1 clove garlic, chopped
2 tablespoons butter
1/2 teaspoon salt
1/8 teaspoon pepper
1 egg, beaten
additional Parmesan cheese, if desired

Spray counter lightly with non-stick cooking spray. Roll loaf or combined dinner rolls into a 12x16-inch rectangle. Cover with plastic wrap and let rest 10-15 minutes. In a bowl, mix cream cheese, spinach, basil, rosemary, egg, Parmesan cheese and ham. Sauté mushrooms, onion, garlic, butter, salt and pepper. Remove wrap from dough.

Spread cream cheese mixture lengthwise in a 4-inch strip down center of dough. Top with mushroom mixture. Make cuts 1 1/2-inches apart on long sides of dough to within 1/2-inch of filling. Begin braid by folding top and bottom strip toward filling. Then braid strips left over right, right over left twisting each strip once. Finish by pulling last strip over and tucking under braid. Lift braid with both hands and place on a large sprayed baking sheet. Brush with beaten egg and sprinkle with Parmesan cheese, if desired. Bake at 350°F 35-45 minutes or until golden brown. Cool slightly and slice to serve.

Cajun Crab Salad

1 loaf Rhodes™ Bread,
  baked following package instructions
garlic salt
5 hard boiled eggs, sliced
1 pound imitation crab,
  separated into bite-sized pieces
5 stalks celery, diced
1/4 cup sliced green onion
1 1/2 cups mayonnaise
1/4 cup finely chopped red pepper
1/4 teaspoon salt
1/4 teaspoon paprika
dash ground cayenne pepper
dash hot sauce

Trim ends off of the loaf of bread. Cut remaining loaf into 1-inch cubes. Place on a baking sheet and sprinkle with garlic salt.

Bake at 350°F 10-15 minutes or until bread begins to crisp. Remove from oven and place in a large mixing bowl to cool.

In a separate mixing bowl, combine remaining ingredients. Stir gently. Add gradually to bread cubes, stirring gently after each addition. Chill and serve cold.

Baked Hot Dogs on a Stick

Rhodes™ Dinner Rolls, thawed but still cold
hot dogs, cut in half
1 egg, beaten
sesame seeds
wooden skewers

Roll one dinner roll into a 10 to12-inch rope. Insert a wooden skewer into each hot dog half. Wrap dough around a hot dog half, tucking ends under dough. Repeat abo steps to make desired amount.

Place on sprayed baking sheets. Brush with beaten egg and sprinkle with sesame see Bake at 375°F 15-20 minutes or until golden brown.

Chicken Verde Loaf

24 Rhodes™ Dinner Rolls,
thawed to room temperature

8 ounces cream cheese,
softened to room temperature

4 ounce can diced green chiles

2.25 ounce can sliced black olives, drained

1/2 cup chopped yellow onion

2-10 ounce cans white chicken, in water,
drained well

Seasoned salt

Pepper

1 tablespoon butter, melted

1/4 cup grated Parmesan cheese

1 tablespoon dried parsley

Spray counter lightly with non-stick cooking spray. Combine rolls together and roll into a 12x18-inch rectangle. Cover with plastic wrap and let rest. In a bowl, combine cream cheese, green chiles, olives and onions until well blended. Add chicken and toss to combine.

Remove wrap and spread chicken mixture evenly over middle third of dough going lengthwise. Sprinkle with salt and pepper. Fold right side over chicken mixture and overlap with left side. Place on sprayed baking sheet, folded side down and tuck ends under. Cover with plastic wrap and let rise 30 minutes.

Remove wrap and brush with butter. Score loaf with a sharp serrated knife then sprinkle with Parmesan cheese and parsley. Bake at 350°F 25-30 minutes. Cover with foil last few minutes of baking, if necessary, to prevent over browning. Slice and serve warm.

Chicken & Swiss Bake

12 Rhodes™ Dinner rolls,
  thawed to room temperature
1/2 cup mayonnaise
1 tablespoon minced fresh parsley
2 teaspoons prepared mustard
2 teaspoons finely chopped onion
2 cups cubed cooked chicken breast
6 bacon strips cooked & crumbled
1 cup grated Swiss cheese

Spray counter lightly with non-stick cooking spray. Combine rolls together and roll into a 12x15-inch rectangle. Cover with plastic wrap and let rest. In a large bowl, combine mayonnaise, parsley, mustard and onion. Stir in the chicken, bacon and cheese.

Remove wrap and spread filling evenly over dough. Starting with a short side, roll up tightly. Pinch edges to seal. Join ends to form a ring and place seam side down on a sprayed baking sheet. With knife or scissors, make cuts nearly to the center of ring 1 1/2 to 2-inches apart. Turn each slice on its side, resting on the adjoining slice. Cover with sprayed plastic wrap and let rise 15-20 minutes. Remove wrap and bake at 375°F 20-25 minutes or until golden brown.

Chili Cheese Braid

Loaf Rhodes™ Bread Dough or 12 Rhodes™
Dinner Rolls, thawed to room temperature
6 ounce can of chili
¼ cup chopped green onions
¼ cup chopped green pepper
cup grated cheddar cheese

Spray counter lightly with non-stick cooking spray. Roll loaf or combined dinner rolls into a 12x16-inch rectangle. Cover with plastic wrap and let rest 10-15 minutes. Remove wrap and pour chili lengthwise in a 4-inch strip down center of dough. Top with green onions, green pepper and cheese. Make cuts 1 ½-inches apart on long sides of dough to within ½-inch of filling. Begin braid by folding top and bottom strips toward filling. Then braid strips left over right, right over left. Finish by pulling last strip over and tucking under braid.

Lift braid with both hands and place on a large sprayed baking sheet. Cover with sprayed plastic wrap and let rise 30 minutes. Remove wrap and bake at 350°F 30-35 minutes or until golden brown. Cool slightly to serve.

Fresh Corn & Cheddar Bake

1 Loaf Rhodes™ Bread, baked following
   instructions on package and day old
2 tablespoons butter
4 cups fresh corn kernels (from 5-6 ears)
1/2 small onion, chopped
1 can diced green chiles
3 large eggs
1 pint half and half
1 tablespoon Dijon mustard
2 teaspoons finely chopped fresh thyme
1 teaspoon salt
1 teaspoon pepper
2 cups grated medium cheddar cheese

Remove crusts from baked loaf, cut into 3/4-inch cubes and set aside. Melt butter in a large skillet over medium high heat. Add corn and onion and cook, stirring often, for about four minutes.

Remove from heat and add green chiles. In a large bowl, whisk together the eggs, half and half, mustard, thyme, salt and pepper. Stir in the corn, onion mixture. Place half of the bread cubes evenly in the bottom of a sprayed 2 1/2 quart casserole dish or 9x13-inch baking dish. Pour in half of the creamy corn mixture. Sprinkle with half of the cheddar cheese. Repeat with the remaining bread, creamy corn mixture and cheese. Bake at 350°F 35-45 minutes.

Chili Cheese Rolls

Rhodes™ Dinner Rolls,
thawed to room temperature
ounce can thick chili
ounces cheddar cheese, cut into 12 cubes

Spray counter lightly with non-stick cooking spray. Combine 2 rolls together and flatten into a 5 to 6-inch circle. Repeat with remaining rolls. In the center of each dough circle, place one cube of cheese and 1-2 tablespoons of thick chili. Fold all edges up over filling and secure with toothpick. Place, seam side up, in a well-sprayed muffin tin. Cover with sprayed plastic wrap and let rise 15-20 minutes. Remove wrap and bake at 350°F 20-25 minutes. Carefully remove to cooling rack. Remove toothpick before serving.

Hamburger Filled Buns

12 Rhodes™ Dinner Rolls,
  thawed to room temperature
1 pound lean ground beef
1/2 cup finely chopped onion
1/2 teaspoon salt
1/4 teaspoon pepper
1/2 teaspoon chili powder
1 teaspoon soy sauce
1 egg, beaten
sesame seeds, if desired

Combine ground beef with onion, salt, pepper, chili powder and soy sauce. Mix well and shape into six 3-inch patties. Fry in skillet, turning once, until cooked. Cool on plate covered with paper towel.

Combine 2 rolls and flatten into an 8-inch circle. Place meat patty in the center of each dough circle. Pull dough up around patty to completely enclose. Pinch together to seal. Place seam side down on a large sprayed baking sheet. Brush with beaten egg and sprinkle with seeds, if desired. Cover with plastic wrap and let rise 15 minutes. Bake at 350°F 20 minutes or until golden brown. Serve warm with ketchup or chili sauce.

Ham, Swiss & Broccoli Braid

1 Loaf Rhodes™ Bread Dough or 12 Rhodes™ Dinner Rolls, thawed to room temperature
2 1/2 cups cooked cubed ham
1 cup fresh broccoli florets
1 1/2 cups grated Swiss cheese
1 cup sliced fresh mushrooms
1/3 cup mayonnaise
1 tablespoon mustard
1/2 teaspoon pepper
1 teaspoon dried basil
1 egg white, beaten
2 tablespoons bread crumbs

Spray counter lightly with non-stick cooking spray. Roll loaf or combined dinner rolls into a 12x16-inch rectangle. Cover with plastic wrap and let rest 10-15 minutes. In a large bowl combine ham, broccoli, cheese, mushrooms, mayonnaise, mustard, pepper and basil and mix well. Remove wrap from dough. Spoon mixture lengthwise in a 4-inch strip down center of dough. Make cuts 1 1/2-inches apart on long sides of dough to within 1/2-inch of filling.    Begin braid by folding top & bottom strips toward filling. Then braid strips left over right, right over left twisting each strip once. Finish by pulling last strip over and tucking under braid. Lift braid with both hands and place on a large sprayed baking sheet. Brush with egg white and sprinkle with bread crumbs. Bake at 350°F 30-35 minutes or until golden brown. Cool slightly and slice to serve.

Italian Sausage Pie

1 Loaf Rhodes™ Bread Dough or 12 Rhodes™ Dinner Rolls, thawed to room temperature
1 pound bulk sausage
1/4 cup chopped yellow onion
1/4 cup thinly sliced sweet red pepper
10 ounce package frozen chopped spinach, thawed & well drained
4 ounce can sliced mushrooms, drained
8 ounce can tomato sauce
1 teaspoon dried basil
1 teaspoon garlic powder
1/2 teaspoon pepper
1/3 cup Italian bread crumbs

Roll 2/3 of loaf (or 8 dinner rolls combined) on a lightly floured surface into a 12-inch circle. Cover with plastic wrap and let rest while preparing filling. In a large skillet, cook sausage until brown. Drain sausage and add onion. Cook for 1-2 minutes. Add red pepper and remove from heat. Add spinach, mushrooms, tomato sauce, basil, garlic powder, pepper and bread crumbs, toss lightly.

Remove wrap and place 12-inch dough circle in a sprayed 10-inch quiche pan or pie plate, covering bottom and up the sides. Add filling. Roll remaining 1/3 loaf (or 4 dinner rolls combined) into an 11-inch circle. Cut circle into 12 wedges. Arrange wedges atop filling, slightly overlapping and sealing edge to bottom crust. Cover with sprayed plastic wrap and let rise 15-20 minutes. Remove wrap and bake at 350°F 30 minutes or until crust is golden brown.

Waffle Sandwiches

Rhodes Texas™ or Dinner Rolls,
thawed to room temperature
peanut butter and jam

Preheat waffle iron to medium high. Flatten each roll into a 4 to 5-inch circle. Spray the waffle iron with non-stick cooking spray. Place a flattened roll in the middle of the waffle iron and close the lid. Cook each roll 1-2 minutes or until light golden brown. Remove and spread with peanut butter and jam.

Ham & Cheese Tart

12 Rhodes™ Dinner Rolls or 8 Rhodes Texas™
   Rolls, thawed to room temperature
4 ounces cream cheese, softened
1/3 cup ricotta cheese
4 tablespoons pesto
2/3 cup chopped, drained sun dried tomatoes
4 ounces ham, chopped
1/4 teaspoon black pepper
1 egg, beaten with 1 tablespoon milk

Combine 6 dinner rolls or 4 Texas™ rolls together and roll out to fit the bottom of a sprayed 10-inch round baking pan. Place dough in pan to cover the bottom and up the sides. In a bowl, mix together the cream cheese, ricotta cheese, and pesto. Place half of the ham over the dough. Next, layer half of the cheese mixture and then half of the tomatoes.

Repeat layers; ham, cheese mixture and tomatoes. Sprinkle with black pepper. Combine remaining 6 dinner rolls or 4 Texas™ rolls. Roll out to fit the top of the tart. Place over tomatoes and pinch edges together to seal. Cut 4 small slits in the top. Brush with egg mixture and bake at 350°F 30-35 minutes.

Braided Athenian Bread

1 Loaf Rhodes™ Bread Dough or
12 Rhodes™ Dinner Rolls,
thawed to room temperature
1 tablespoon fresh minced garlic
1 ounce can whole black olives, halved
1/4 cup chopped Italian parsley
2 tablespoons capers, drained
1/4 cup sliced sundried tomatoes
1/4 cup sour cream
1 teaspoon black pepper
1/4 cup grated Parmesan cheese
1 egg, beaten
poppy seeds

Spray counter lightly with non-stick cooking spray. Roll loaf or combined dinner rolls into a 12x16-inch rectangle. Cover with plastic wrap and let rest 10-15 minutes. In a bowl, combine garlic, olives, parsley, capers, tomatoes, sour cream and pepper.

Remove wrap from dough and spread filling lengthwise in a 4-inch strip down center of dough. Sprinkle filling with Parmesan cheese. Make cuts 1/2-inches apart on long sides of dough to within 1/2-inch of filling. Begin braid by folding top and bottom strips toward filling. Then braid strips left over right, right over left. Finish by pulling last strip over and tucking under braid.

Lift braid with both hands and place on a large sprayed baking sheet. Brush with beaten egg and sprinkle with poppy seeds. Cover with sprayed plastic wrap and let rise 30 minutes. Remove wrap and bake at 350°F 25-30 minutes or until golden brown. Cool slightly and slice to serve.

Ham & Cheese Stromboli

1 Loaf Rhodes™ Bread Dough,
 thawed to room temperature
1/2 pound sliced Swiss cheese
1/2 pound thinly sliced deli ham
1 cup grated cheddar cheese
1 cup grated mozzarella cheese
2 cups fresh broccoli florets, lightly steamed
1/2 teaspoon garlic powder
1/2 teaspoon dried basil
1/2 teaspoon black pepper
flour

On a lightly floured surface, roll dough into an 18x12-inch rectangle. Layer dough with Swiss cheese, ham, cheddar cheese, mozzarella cheese and broccoli to within 1-inch of edges. Sprinkle with garlic powder, basil and pepper. Roll up jelly-roll style, starting with a long side. Seal seams and ends. Place seam side down on a large, sprayed baking sheet. Make 1/4-inch deep diagonal slits, about every 1 1/2-inches, with a sharp serrated knife, if desired. Dust top with flour. Cover with sprayed plastic wrap and let rise 30 minutes. Remove wrap and bake at 375°F 20 minutes. Cover loosely with foil and bake an additional 20 minutes. Let stand 10 minutes before slicing.

Tomato Basil Tart

Rhodes™ Dinner Rolls,
 thawed to room temperature
1/2 cups grated fresh Parmesan cheese
1/2 cups grated Gruyere cheese
tablespoons chopped fresh basil
-4 medium size tomatoes, sliced
alt & fresh ground pepper
-2 tablespoons olive oil

Spray counter lightly with non-stick cooking spray. Combine rolls and roll into a 12-inch circle. Place on a large sprayed baking sheet. In a bowl, combine cheeses and basil.

Spread cheese mixture evenly over dough, leaving a 2-3-inch border all around. Top with sliced tomatoes and salt and pepper. Fold the 2-3-inch border of dough up over filling, pleating as you work your way around the tart. Brush crust with olive oil and secure in a few spots with toothpicks if necessary. Bake at 325°F 35-40 minutes.

Italian Panini

18 Rhodes™ Dinner Rolls,
  thawed to room temperature
bottled pesto
8 slices provolone cheese
spinach leaves
sliced pepperoni
roasted bell peppers, cut into thin strips
8-12 slices deli turkey breast
olive oil
dried basil

Spray counter lightly with non-stick cooking spray. Combine rolls together and roll into a 12x18-inch rectangle. Place on a sprayed 11x17-inch baking sheet. Let rise 30 minutes. Press dough down with fingers to make a dimpled surface. Bake at 350°F 15-20 minutes or until lightly browned. Remove from oven and place on cooling rack. While still warm, cut into 8 equal pieces to make 4 panini sandwiches. Spread 2 pieces, lightly, with pesto. Top one with one slice cheese, spinach leaves, sliced pepperoni, roasted bell pepper strips, 2-3 slices turkey and another slice of cheese. Place remaining bread, pesto side down, on top. Repeat with remaining bread pieces.

Brush both sides of sandwich with olive oil and sprinkle with dried basil. Heat skillet over medium low heat until hot. Place sandwich in skillet. Place smaller skillet on top of sandwich and press down to flatten slightly (or use a panini grill). Cook 1-2 minutes on each side. Repeat with remaining sandwiches.

Stroganoff Loaf

2 Rhodes™ Dinner Rolls,
thawed to room temperature
1 pound lean ground beef
1/2 cup chopped onion
2 garlic cloves, minced
1 tablespoon butter
1 1/2 cups sliced fresh mushrooms
8 ounces cream cheese
2 tablespoons chopped fresh basil
Salt & pepper to taste

Combine rolls and roll into a 10x18-inch rectangle. Cover with plastic wrap and let rest. Brown hamburger and drain well. Add onion and garlic to hamburger and cook until onions are clear. Melt butter in a small pan. Add mushrooms and saute for a few minutes. Add mushrooms, cream cheese and basil to hamburger mixture. Salt and pepper to taste.

Remove wrap and spread mixture evenly over middle third of dough going lengthwise. Fold 18-inch sides over meat mixture. Tuck ends under. Place on a large sprayed baking sheet. Cover again with sprayed plastic wrap and let rise 30 minutes. Remove wrap and make 1/4-inch deep diagonal slits, about every 1 1/2-inches, with a sharp serrated knife, if desired. Bake at 350°F 25-30 minutes.

Burger Bites (Sliders)

Rhodes™ Dinner Rolls, thawed but still cold
lean ground beef
favorite burger toppings

Cut each dinner roll in half and shape into a small bun. Place on sprayed baking sheets about 2-inches apart. Cover with sprayed plastic wrap and let rise until double in size. Remove wrap and bake at 350°F 15-20 minutes or until golden brown. Make patties out of lean ground beef to fit the buns, about 2 to 2¹/2-inches in diameter. Slice cooled buns in half and fill with a cooked patty and your favorite burger toppings.

Stuffed Reuben Pie

12 Rhodes™ Dinner Rolls,
 thawed to room temperature
tablespoons prepared Thousand Island dressing
1/2 cups grated Swiss cheese, divided
pound deli pastrami
cup sauerkraut, well drained
tablespoon olive oil
caraway seeds

Spray counter lightly with non-stick cooking spray. Combine 6 rolls together and roll into an 10-inch circle. Cover with plastic wrap and let rest about 10 minutes. Repeat the above steps with remaining 6 rolls. Remove wrap from dough circles and place one circle in a sprayed 9-inch round baking pan covering the bottom and 1/2-inch up the sides. Spread Thousand Island dressing evenly over dough. Top with 1/2 of the cheese. Arrange the pastrami evenly over the cheese. Top with sauerkraut and sprinkle with remaining cheese. Place remaining dough circle over the top and pinch the edges together to seal to the bottom dough circle. Brush with olive oil and sprinkle with caraway seeds. Cut 2-3 vents in the center. Bake at 375°F 35-40 minutes. Cover with foil last 10 minutes, if necessary, to prevent over browning.

Rhodes
Classic
Recipe

Gourmet Turkey Rolls

Rhodes Classic Recipe

12 Rhodes Texas™ Rolls,
   thawed but still cold
2 tablespoons butter or margarine
½ cup onion, chopped
8 ounces fresh mushrooms, sliced
½ pound sausage, uncooked
½ teaspoon sage
½ teaspoon marjoram
⅛ teaspoon allspice
1 egg, separated
1 pound cooked turkey, cubed
whole sage leaves

In a skillet, melt butter. Saute onions
and mushrooms and set aside. In a
bowl, combine uncooked sausage,
sage, marjoram, allspice and egg yolk.
Mix well. Add turkey and onion
mixture. Combine two rolls and
flatten into an 8-inch circle, prepare
6 circles. Divide turkey mixture evenly
between the circles. Fold dough over
filling and pinch ends together.

Place pinched-side down on a large
sprayed baking sheet. Brush with
beaten egg white. Place 3 whole sage
leaves on top, if desired, and brush
again. Bake at 375°F 30-35
minutes or until golden brown.

Football Hero Sandwich

Rhodes™ Dinner Rolls,
thawed to room temperature
egg, beaten
mayonnaise, if desired
lettuce leaves
slices deli ham
slices cheese

Cut 1/2 of one roll off and roll it into a 10-inch rope. Cut this rope into 4 segments to be used for the ball laces. Set aside. Press the remaining 5 1/2 rolls into a football shape,  leaving the top mounded and edges thinner. Pull the ends to exaggerate the points. Place on a baking sheet sprayed with non-stick cooking spray. With a knife, make a slight cut across the top of the football, not quite reaching the points. Lay each lace across the cut. Using a toothpick or knife, push the ends of the laces down into the football securing them tightly. Brush with egg and let rise for 30 minutes. Bake at 350°F 20 minutes or until golden brown. Let cool and then slice. Spread with mayonnaise, if desired, and stuff with lettuce, deli meat and cheese.

Philly Stuffed Pies

6 Rhodes Texas™ White or Wheat Rolls or 12 Rhodes™
  Dinner Rolls, thawed to room temperature
1 pound package pre-cooked beef roast au jus
1 tablespoon butter
1 medium size yellow onion, sliced thin
1 medium size green pepper, chopped
8 ounces fresh sliced mushrooms
6 ounces sliced provolone cheese
shredded fresh Parmesan cheese

Using 1 Texas roll or 2 combined dinner rolls, flatten into 6 to 7-inch circles.
Heat roast beef following instructions on package. Remove from au jus and set
aside. Melt butter in skillet. Add onion, green pepper and mushrooms and cook
until tender. Shred roast beef and divide evenly between the 6 dough circles.

Top with equally divided onion mixture and provolone cheese. Fold roll in half
over filling, like a turnover. Press and seal edges together with a fork. Brush the
top of each stuffed pie with a little water and sprinkle with shredded Parmesan
cheese. Place on a sprayed baking sheet and bake at 350°F 20-25 minutes.
If desired, serve au jus as a dip with pies.

Runzas (Bierocks)

12 Rhodes Texas™ Rolls, or 24 Rhodes™ Dinner
Rolls, thawed but still cold
4 cups sliced cabbage
1 cup sliced yellow onion
1 tablespoon vegetable oil
8 ounces ground beef
1 teaspoon sugar
1 tablespoon vinegar
1 teaspoon salt
1 teaspoon pepper
1 cup mozzarella cheese, grated
2 tablespoons butter, melted

Saute cabbage and onion in oil. Cover and steam for 30 minutes. Brown ground beef in a large pan, and drain well. Add cabbage, onion, sugar, vinegar, salt and pepper and cook for an additional 10 minutes.

Flatten each Texas™ roll, or 2 dinner rolls into a 6-inch circle. Divide filling among 12 circles (about 1/3 cup). Place 1 tablespoon mozzarella cheese on top of filling. Pull edges around filling and pinch to close.

Place on a large sprayed baking sheet, pinched side down. Brush tops with melted butter. Bake at 350°F 30-35 minutes.

Braided Spaghetti Bread

1 Loaf Rhodes™ Bread Dough or 12 Rhodes™
  Dinner Rolls, thawed to room temperature
6 ounces spaghetti, cooked
1 cup thick spaghetti sauce
8 ounces mozzarella cheese,
  cut into ½-inch cubes
1 egg white, beaten
Parmesan cheese
parsley flakes

Spray counter lightly with non-stick cooking spray. Roll loaf or combined dinner rolls into a 12x16-inch rectangle. Cover with plastic wrap and let rest 10-15 minutes. Cook spaghetti according to package instructions. Drain and let cool slightly. Remove wrap from dough. Place spaghetti lengthwise in a 4-inch strip down center of dough. Top with sauce and cheese cubes. Make cuts 1 ½-inches apart on long sides of dough to within ½-inch of filling. Begin braid by folding top and bottom strips toward filling. Then braid strips left over right, right over left. Finish by pulling last strip over and tucking under braid. Lift braid with both hands and place on a large sprayed baking sheet. Brush with egg white and sprinkle with Parmesan cheese and parsley. Bake at 350°F 30-35 minutes or until golden brown. Cool slightly and slice to serve.

Campfire Twirly Dogs

Rhodes™ Dinner Rolls, thawed
  but still cold (one per hot dog)
hot dogs

Roll each roll into a 12-inch rope. Wrap the rope around a hot dog 2 or 3 times, securing ends in dough.

Place each Twirly Dog on a roasting stick. Cook over campfire or coals, turning often, about 20 minutes or until dough is cooked and browned. Serve with your favorite hot dog fixin's.

Can also be baked in 350°F oven 15-20 minutes.

133

Sweets Treats

These yummy desserts are
easy to make and delicious
to eat.

Butterscotch Bubble Loaf

24 Rhodes™ Dinner Rolls, thawed but still cold
½ box butterscotch or vanilla pudding mix,
non-instant
½ cup pecans, chopped
½ cup brown sugar
½ cup butter or margarine

Cut dinner rolls in half and dip in dry pudding mix. Arrange rolls in sprayed bundt pan alternately with pecans. Sprinkle any remaining pudding mix over the top. Combine brown sugar and butter. Heat together until butter is melted and a syrup is formed (microwave about 1 ½ minutes). Pour syrup over rolls.

Cover with sprayed plastic wrap. Let rise until double in size or even with top of bundt pan. Carefully remove wrap. Bake at 350°F 30-35 minutes. Cover with foil the last 15 minutes of baking. Immediately after baking, loosen from sides of the pan with a knife and invert onto a serving plate.

Cranberry Cream Cheese Pull-Aparts

24 Rhodes™ Dinner Rolls, thawed but still cold
3 ounces dried cranberries
1/4 cup butter, melted
1 cup granulated sugar (divided)
3/4 cup (6 ounces) cream cheese, softened
3 tablespoons fresh orange juice
1 tablespoon each grated orange rind and lemon rind
1 cup powdered sugar
2 teaspoons fresh lemon juice

Press about 1 teaspoon cranberries into each thawed roll. Place rolls in a 9x13-inch sprayed baking pan. Combine the butter, 1/2 cup sugar, cream cheese, and orange juice. Blend well and pour over the rolls. Cover with sprayed plastic wrap and let rise until double in size.

Combine 1/2 cup sugar, the rinds and any remaining cranberries. Remove wrap and sprinkle the mixture over the risen rolls. Bake immediately in preheated 350°F oven 25 minutes or until rolls in center are done.

Combine powdered sugar and lemon juice and drizzle over rolls

Fresh Fruit Pizza

9 Rhodes™ Dinner Rolls
  or 6 Rhodes Texas™ Rolls,
  thawed to room temperature
1-2 tablespoons milk
1-2 tablespoons sugar
8 ounces strawberry cream cheese spread
1 cup whipped topping
fresh fruit as desired

Spray counter lightly with non-stick
cooking spray. Combine rolls together
and roll into a 13-inch circle. Place on
a sprayed 12-inch pizza pan. Build up
edges slightly.

Brush with milk and sprinkle with
sugar. Poke crust several times with
a fork to prevent air bubbles from
forming.

Bake at 350°F 10-15 minutes until
light golden brown. Set aside to cool.
Combine cream cheese spread and
whipped topping and mix well.
Spread over cooled crust. Top with
your favorite fresh fruits.

Cinnamon Blueberry Crumble

Rhodes Anytime!™ Cinnamon Rolls
ounce can blueberry pie filling
cup butter, softened
cup flour
cup brown sugar
cup chopped pecans
am cheese frosting (included with
Anytime!™ Cinnamon Rolls)

Remove rolls from pan. Spray pan with non-stick cooking spray and replace rolls. Spread blueberry pie filling evenly over and between rolls.

Combine butter, flour, brown sugar and pecans and sprinkle over pie filling. Place pan on a large baking sheet to catch any drips. Bake at 350°F 45-50 minutes. Drizzle with cream cheese frosting while still warm.

Southern Peach Cobbler

6 Rhodes AnyTime!™ Cinnamon Rolls,
  thawed but still cold
21 ounce can peach pie filling
whipped cream, if desired

Remove rolls from the pan or bag they come in. Cut each roll into 4 equal pieces and set aside. Spray pie pan with non-stick cooking spray, then spread pie filling evenly in the pan. Arrange the cinnamon roll pieces on top of the pie filling to cover evenly. Bake at 350°F 25-30 minutes. Serve warm with whipped cream, if desired.

Caramel Pecan Knots

Rhodes Texas™ Rolls,
thawed but still cold
¼ cup pecan pieces
½ cup brown sugar
¼ cup heavy cream
½ teaspoon cinnamon
¼ cup sugar

Roll each roll into a 10-inch rope
and tie in a knot. Set aside and
cover with sprayed plastic wrap.
Spread pecans over the bottom of
a sprayed 10-inch round baking
pan. Sprinkle brown sugar evenly
over pecans. Carefully pour
cream over sugar and pecans.
Mix cinnamon and sugar in a
shallow bowl.

Remove wrap from rolls and dip
each one into cinnamon and
sugar mixture. Place in the round
baking pan, putting one in center
and 7 around the outside. Cover
with the sprayed plastic wrap
again and let rise until double.
Remove wrap and bake at 350°F
30-35 minutes. Remove from
oven and invert onto serving
platter.

143

Pani Popo
Coconut Rolls

18 Rhodes™ Dinner Rolls
14 ounce can coconut cream or milk
1/2 cup sugar

Place frozen rolls in 3 rows of 6 in a sprayed 9x13-inch baking dish. Cover with sprayed plastic wrap and let thaw and rise until double in size. Combine coconut cream and sugar and mix well.

Remove wrap from risen rolls and pour coconut cream mixture over the rolls (try to coat each roll completely as you pour so they will have a consistent color as they bake.) Bake at 350°F 30-35 minutes.

Note: Coconut cream mixture will thicken as the rolls cool.

Bananas Foster Medallions

12 Rhodes™ Dinner Rolls,
 thawed to room temperature
3 tablespoons butter
1/2 cup brown sugar
4 bananas, cut into 1/2-inch chunks
1 egg, lightly beaten
Oil for deep frying

Preheat oil to 350°F, enough that the 3-inch medallions can float freely. Spray counter lightly with non-stick spray. Cut each roll in half and flatten each half into a 3-inch circle. Cover with plastic wrap and let rest. Melt butter in a skillet. Add brown sugar and heat to a low boil. Cook at this temperature for five minutes, stirring constantly (butter and sugar may not combine completely). Add bananas and continue to cook at a low boil. Mixture will be thin. Stir constantly until mixture thickens. Remove from heat to cool.

Remove wrap from dough circles. Brush 12 of the circles, around edges, with the beaten egg. Divide cooled banana filling equally between the remaining 12 dough circles. Top with the 12 egg washed dough circles, egg washed side down, and pinch together to seal completely. Before deep frying, pinch edges together once more. Fry in small batches until deep golden brown on both sides. Place on a rack to drain. Serve warm with vanilla ice cream, if desired.

Caramel Apple Twist

16 Rhodes™ Dinner Rolls,
 thawed to room temperature
2 large Granny Smith apples,
 peeled, cored and chopped
12 caramel cubes, cut into fourths
1/2 cup brown sugar
3/4 cup chopped almonds, divided
1 tablespoon cinnamon
2 tablespoons flour
1/2 cup prepared vanilla icing

Spray counter lightly with non-stick cooking spray. Combine 8 dinner rolls and roll into a 6x16-inch rectangle. Repeat with remaining rolls. Cover with plastic wrap and let rest. In a large bowl combine apples, caramels, brown sugar, 1/2 cup almonds, cinnamon and flour. Remove wrap from dough. Divide apple mixture equally between the two rectangles and spread down the center of each rectangle. Fold both edges of each rectangle over the filling, overlapping slightly, and pinch together to seal.

Place both filled rectangles on a sprayed baking sheet and carefully twist them together. Press ends together. Cover with sprayed plastic wrap and let rise 15-20 minutes. Remove wrap and bake at 350°F 25-30 minutes or until lightly browned. Cool slightly. Microwave vanilla icing for 10 seconds. Drizzle over twist and sprinkle with remaining 1/4 cup of almonds.

Chocolate Stuffed Sticky Bundt

4 Rhodes™ Dinner Rolls, thawed but still cold
1/2 cups milk chocolate chips
2 cup granulated sugar
 tablespoon cocoa
 teaspoon ground cinnamon
2 cup chopped pecans or toffee bits
2 cup butter or margarine, melted
2 cup packed brown sugar

Cut rolls in half and flatten each half. Wrap each half around 1 teaspoon chocolate chips and completely enclose. In a bowl, mix granulated sugar, cocoa and cinnamon. Dip each roll half in sugar mixture until well coated. Place in a large sprayed bundt pan. Sprinkle any remaining sugar mixture along with pecans or toffee bits over rolls. Combine butter and brown sugar in a small bowl and microwave 30 seconds. Stir well and pour over rolls.

Cover with plastic wrap and let rise until almost to the top of the pan. Remove wrap and bake at 350°F 35 minutes. Cover with foil last 10 minutes of baking. Invert immediately onto serving platter.

White Chocolate Almond Bread Pudding

5 cups Rhodes™ White Bread, baked and cut into 1-inch cubes (day old)
2 cups half and half
1 tablespoon almond extract
1 tablespoon vanilla
2 eggs
1/2 cup sugar
1 cup white chocolate chips, melted
raspberry sauce, if desired

Raspberry Sauce:
2 cups frozen raspberries
3/4 cup sugar
1 tablespoon cornstarch
1/8 teaspoon salt
1/2 cup fresh raspberries

Place bread cubes in a large mixing bowl. Combine half and half, almond extract and vanilla. Pour over bread cubes, stirring gently to soak bread. Beat together eggs and sugar. Add melted chips. Fold into bread mixture.

Pour into an 8-inch sprayed square pan. Bake at 350°F 50-60 minutes, or until a knife inserted in pudding comes out clean. Serve slices with raspberry sauce.

Raspberry Sauce:
Place frozen raspberries in pan to heat and add 1/2 cup sugar. Bring to a boil and add remaining dry ingredients. Cook until clear and thick. Strain to remove seeds, if desired. Cool and add fresh raspberries.

Blueberry Cream Cheese Crumb Cake

12 Rhodes™ Dinner Rolls,
thawed to room temperature

Filling:
1/2 cup butter or margarine, softened
1/2 cup sugar
2 eggs
6 ounces cream cheese, softened
1/4 cup cornstarch
1 tablespoon grated lemon peel
1 cup frozen blueberries, thawed

Topping:
1 cup flour
1/4 cup sugar
pinch of salt
3 tablespoons butter, softened

Combine rolls and roll into a 12x17-inch rectangle. Cover with plastic wrap and let rest. To make filling, cream butter and sugar in a medium bowl until light and fluffy. Beat in eggs, cream cheese, cornstarch, and lemon peel.

Uncover dough and place in a sprayed jelly roll pan (10x15-inch) to cover bottom and sides. Spread cream cheese mixture over dough. Top with blueberries. To make topping, mix flour, sugar, and salt in a medium bowl.

Gradually add butter to flour mixture using a fork. Mixture should resemble crumbs. Sprinkle crumb topping over filling and blueberries. Let stand 15 minutes. Bake at 350°F 45-50 minutes.

Cranberry Orange Pull-Apart

12 Rhodes™ Orange Rolls
  or 24 Rhodes™ Dinner Rolls*
  thawed but still cold
small package non-instant vanilla pudding
1/4 cup dried cranberries
1 orange rind, grated
1/2 cup butter or margarine, melted
cream cheese frosting, included with orange rolls

Cut rolls in half and roll in dry pudding mix. Arrange, alternately with cranberries and orange rind, in large sprayed bundt pan. Sprinkle remaining pudding over rolls. Pour melted butter over top. Cover with plastic wrap and let rise until double in size. Remove wrap and bake at 350°F 30-35 minutes. Cover with foil last 15 minutes of baking. Remove from oven and immediately invert onto a serving platter. Cool slightly and drizzle with cream cheese frosting.

*If using dinner rolls, add 1/4 cup sugar to pudding and follow recipe above. For frosting, mix 1 cup powdered sugar, l tablespoon melted butter and 2 tablespoons fresh orange juice.

Crunchy Caramel Chocolate Sticks

Rhodes™ Dinner Rolls, thawed but still cold
ounce package caramels, melted
small package milk chocolate chips, melted
small package white chocolate chips, melted

Cut each roll in half and roll into a 10-inch stick. Place on a large sprayed baking sheet. Do not allow sticks to touch as you want the breadsticks to be crispy all around. Bake at 400°F 15-20 minutes or until golden brown. Cool completely (let sticks sit out overnight to make them crispier).

Dip about two thirds of each breadstick in melted caramel. Place back on sprayed cookie sheet and cool in refrigerator until completely set. Remove from refrigerator and bring to room temperature. Drizzle with melted chocolate as desired.

Chocolate Pecan Rolls

1 Loaf Rhodes™ Bread Dough or 12 Rhodes™
    Dinner Rolls, thawed to room temperature
2 tablespoons butter or margarine, melted
1/4 cup brown sugar
1/4 cup butter or margarine
2 tablespoons light corn syrup
1/2 cup chocolate chips
1/3 cup brown sugar
1/2 cup chopped pecans

Spray counter lightly with non-stick cooking spray. Roll loaf or combined
dinner rolls into a 12x16-inch rectangle. Brush dough with melted butter.
Combine 1/4 cup brown sugar, 1/4 cup butter and corn syrup in a small
saucepan and melt until sugar dissolves. Spread evenly over dough.
Combine chocolate chips, 1/3 cup brown sugar and pecans and spread
over dough. Roll up jelly roll style, starting with a 16-inch side.
With sharp serrated knife cut into 12 pieces. Place in a 9x13-inch
sprayed pan. Cover with sprayed plastic wrap and let rise until double.
Remove wrap and bake at 350°F 15-20 minutes.

Mini Monkey Bread

Rhodes™ Dinner rolls,
thawed but still cold
tablespoons butter, melted
tablespoons corn syrup
cup brown sugar
teaspoons cinnamon

ng:
cup powdered sugar
ablespoon butter, melted
2 tablespoons milk
teaspoon vanilla

ut each dinner roll into 6 equal
eces. In a bowl, combine butter
d corn syrup and stir until well
ixed. In another bowl, combine
gar and cinnamon and mix well.
ip 6 roll pieces at a time in the
tter mixture and then in the
gar mixture. Place these 6 pieces
each well-sprayed cup of a
- cup muffin tin.

over with sprayed plastic wrap
d let double in size. Remove
ap and bake at 350°F 15-20
nutes. Cool 3-4 minutes before
moving from pan. Combine
ng ingredients and mix well.
rizzle over monkey breads,
desired.

Pumpkin Pear Bread Pudding

1 loaf Rhodes™ Bread Dough, baked and cut
  into 1-inch cubes (day old)
2 eggs
15 ounce can pumpkin
1 cup canned pears, drained and chopped
14 ounce can sweetened condensed milk
$1/2$ cup sugar
$1/2$ tablespoon nutmeg
$1/2$ tablespoon ginger
$1/2$ tablespoon ground cloves
1 teaspoon cinnamon

Streusel:
1 cup coarsely chopped pecans
$1/2$ teaspoon cinnamon
2 tablespoons flour
2 tablespoons butter
$1/2$ cup brown sugar

In a large mixing bowl, beat eggs.
Add pumpkin, pears, milk, sugar and
spices and mix well. Gently stir in
bread cubes until completely coated.
Pour into a 9-inch sprayed square
baking dish or spring form pan.
Cover and refrigerate 1-2 hours
(may be refrigerated overnight).

Just before baking, combine streusel
ingredients and mix well. Sprinkle
mixture over bread pudding. Bake at
350°F 40-45 minutes or until knife
inserted in center comes out clean.
Serve while still warm, with a
dollop of whipped cream.

Cinnamon Apple Crumble

Rhodes Anytime!™ Cinnamon Rolls,
thawed but still cold
ounces apple pie filling

pping:
cup sugar
cup flour
cup butter, softened

Remove thawed cinnamon rolls from pan and place on a cutting board. Top rolls with apple pie filling. Using a sharp knife, cut rolls and pie filling into small pieces until well combined. Spray pan with non-stick cooking spray. Place cut up rolls and pie filling back in pan.

For topping: combine sugar and flour. Mix in butter until mixture is crumbly. Sprinkle over rolls and apple pie filling. Bake at 350°F 40-45 minutes.

Petal Pull-Aparts

12 Rhodes™ Dinner Rolls, thawed but still cold
non-stick, butter-flavored cooking spray
1 lemon peel, grated
1/3 cup sugar
3-4 tablespoons raspberry jam or pie filling

Glaze:
1/2 cup powdered sugar
1/2 teaspoon vanilla
1 tablespoon butter, melted
4-5 tablespoons hot water

Combine two rolls into one ball to form the center of flower. Place in the center of a large sprayed baking sheet. Shape remaining rolls into petals and place around center, allowing room for them to rise. Spray well with butter-flavored spray. Cover with plastic wrap. Let rise until double, about one hour. Remove wrap and spray again. Mix lemon peel with sugar and sprinkle over all. Depress center of each petal with your finger and spoon in about one teaspoon jam or pie filling. Bake at 350°F 15-20 minutes or until golden brown. Remove from pan while still warm. Mix glaze ingredients and drizzle over flower.

Dutch Oven Caramel Apple Pie

8 Rhodes AnyTime!™ Cinnamon Rolls,
thawed but still cold
Granny Smith apples, peeled and
sliced
1/2 cup brown sugar
teaspoon cinnamon
1/2 cup graham cracker crumbs
1/4 cup chopped pecans

Caramel Icing
packets cream cheese frosting
(included with rolls)
1/3 cup caramel ice cream topping

Cut each roll into 4 pieces and
arrange in the bottom of a
14-inch Dutch oven lined with
aluminum foil or sprayed with
non-stick cooking spray. In a
bowl, combine apples, brown
sugar, cinnamon, cracker
crumbs and pecans. Sprinkle
evenly over cut rolls. Cover
with lid and bake at 350°F
25-30 minutes.

For icing, combine cream
cheese frosting with caramel
topping. Drizzle over pie while
still warm.

For Dutch oven temperature
control using briquets:
Achieve about 350°F in a
14-inch Dutch oven by using
8 on top, 10 on the bottom.

Holidays

Try something new.
Make a memorable holiday
for your family and
friends.

Valentine Dinner Rolls

12 Rhodes™ Dinner Rolls,
thawed but still cold

Roll each roll into a 4-inch drumstick shape (skinny on one end and fat on the other).

Cut into the fat end about 1 1/2-inches. Place on a sprayed baking sheet pulling the cut pieces apart and laying them cut side down on the baking sheet to form the top of the heart.

Slightly flatten heart shape. (The shape you originally create will fill out and distort while rising so defining characteristics should be emphasized.

Cover with sprayed plastic wrap and let rise until double. Remove wrap and bake at 350°F 15-20 minutes.

Melt Your Heart Pizza

Rhodes Texas™ Rolls
or 9 Rhodes™ Dinner Rolls,
  thawed to room temperature
¼ to ½ cup pizza sauce
 cup grated mozzarella cheese
-10 slices pepperoni, cut into heart shapes
iced olives

Spray counter lightly with non-stick cooking spray. Combine rolls together and roll into a 12 to 14-inch heart shape. Place on a large sprayed pizza pan or baking sheet.

Cover with sprayed plastic wrap and let rise 20-30 minutes. Remove wrap and poke several times with a fork. Pre-bake at 350°F 8-10 minutes. Remove from oven and let cool slightly. Spread crust with pizza sauce and top with cheese, pepperoni and olives. Return to oven and bake until cheese is melted.

179

Cinna-Bunnies

6 Rhodes Anytime™ Cinnamon Rolls,
   thawed but still cold
cream cheese frosting (included with rolls)
candy to decorate face
sliced almonds for teeth

Place three rolls on a
sprayed baking sheet for
the bunny heads (leave
space around rolls for the
ears). Unwind the other
three rolls and fold both
ends toward the center.

Place above head for ears. Bake at 350°F 20-25 minutes. Remove from oven and allow
to cool. Frost with cream cheese frosting and decorate face as desired with different
candies and sliced almonds for teeth.

Ducky Dinner Rolls

16 Rhodes™ Dinner Rolls,
  thawed but still cold
1 egg, beaten
sliced almonds

Slightly flatten 12 rolls and form them each into a teardrop shape. Place on a sprayed baking sheet. Pinch the pointed ends to make tails and press your finger into the rounded end of each teardrop to make a deep hole.

Cut the remaining 4 rolls into thirds. Shape each third into a ball with a pointed end. Dip pointed ends in water and insert into the finger hole on the body for the head.

Brush well with beaten egg. Cover with sprayed plastic wrap and let rise 30 minutes. Remove wrap and pinch tails again. Bake at 350°F 15-20 minutes. Remove from oven, make a small slit with a sharp knife and insert a sliced almond for the duck bill.

181

Easter Egg Dinner Rolls

12 Rhodes™ Dinner Rolls,
  thawed but still cold
egg yolks
food coloring

Flatten each dinner roll into an egg shape and place on a sprayed baking sheet. (The shape you originally create will fill out and distort while rising, so make sure you emphasize the defining characteristics.)

Cover with sprayed plastic wrap and let rise until almost double in size. Mix egg yolks with food coloring to get desired colors. Remove wrap from rolls and paint with colore egg yolk as desired. Bake at 350°F 15-20 minutes.

unny Buns

Rhodes™ Dinner Rolls, thawed but still cold

Cut a small piece off of one roll for a tail. Roll remaining piece into a 12-inch rope with pointed ends. Twist top of rope together. Place on a large sprayed baking sheet and pull pointed ends apart for ears. Roll small cut off piece into a ball for the tail. Make an indentation with your finger at the spot for the tail. Moisten the tail with water and place in the indentation. Repeat the above steps with remaining rolls. Cover with sprayed plastic wrap and allow to rise 30-45 minutes. Remove wrap and bake at 350°F 15-20 minutes or until golden brown. Enjoy with butter for your Easter Dinner.

Cranberry Hot Cross Buns

18 Rhodes™ Dinner rolls, thawed but still cold
3/4 cup dried cranberries

Frosting:
1 1/3 cups powdered sugar
1 1/2 teaspoons lemon zest
1 teaspoon lemon juice
1-2 tablespoons milk

Cut 6 rolls in half. Press 1 1/2 rolls into a flat circle. Put 1 tablespoon of cranberries on roll and bring edges together, mixing berries into the dough. Shape into a round roll. Place on a large sprayed baking sheet. Repeat directions for additional rolls.

Cover with sprayed plastic wrap and let double in size. Remove wrap and bake at 350°F 20 minutes or until golden brown. Let cool. Mix ingredients for frosting and frost rolls.

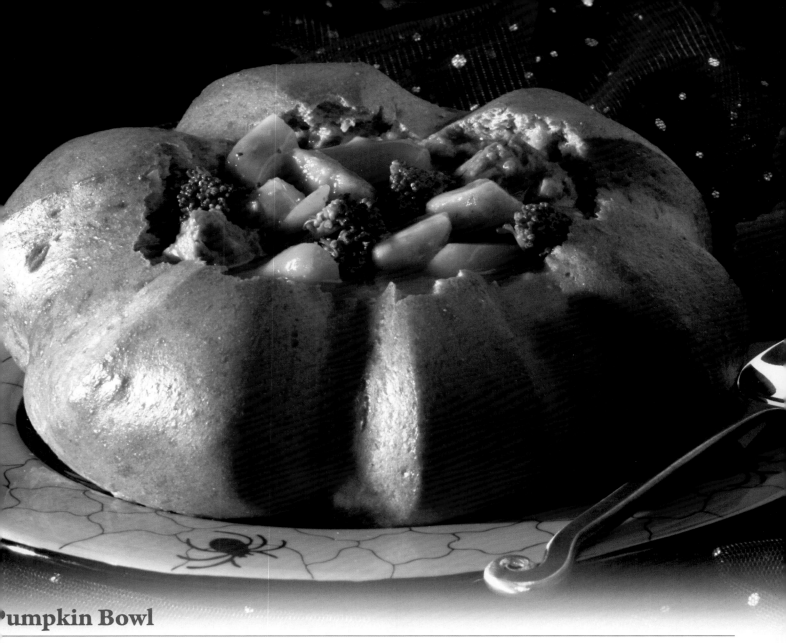

Pumpkin Bowl

Loaf Rhodes™ Wheat
or White Bread dough, thawed but still cold
egg, beaten

Cut off a small piece of dough to use for a stem and set aside. Shape remaining dough into a round ball. With a knife, cut the ball from top to bottom (1/2 inch deep) 6 times to imitate pumpkin sections.

Using the handle of a wooden spoon, poke a deep hole into the top of the bowl down to the base. Shape the small piece that was cut off into a cone and insert the small end into the hole. Place on a sprayed baking sheet and brush with egg. Cover with plastic wrap and let rise until double. Remove wrap and bake at 350°F 20-30 minutes. Let cool, then cut off the top. Hollow out the pumpkin and fill with your favorite stew, dip, chili or soup. For 2 smaller pumpkin bowls, cut loaf in half widthwise and follow instructions above.

Bone Chillin' Breadsticks

12 Rhodes™ Dinner Rolls, thawed but still cold
1/4 cup butter, melted
Parmesan cheese
poppy seeds

Halloween Dip:
1 pound lean ground beef
1 pound processed cheese, Mexican style
10 ounce can diced tomatoes with green
  chilies, undrained
4 ounce can diced green chilies, undrained

Using the flat of your hand, roll the center part of a roll into a 6-inch rope leaving both ends large and rounded. With scissors, clip 1 1/2 inches into the center of each end. Separate and lay the cut sides flat on a large sprayed baking sheet. They will look like bones. Brush well with melted butter and sprinkle with Parmesan cheese and poppy seeds.

Cover with plastic wrap and let rise about 20-30 minutes. Remove wrap and bake at 350°F 15-20 minutes. Serve with Halloween Dip, if desired.

Halloween Dip: In a frying pan, brown ground beef until completely cooked. Drain and set aside. Cut cheese into 1-inch cubes and place in microwave safe bowl. Microwave until melted. Add tomatoes and green chilies and mix well. Combine cooked ground beef with cheese mixture and serve warm.

Happy Jack Pizza

Rhodes™ Dinner Rolls,
thawed to room temperature
cup pizza sauce
pound ground sausage, cooked and drained
cups grated cheddar cheese
green pepper
ami or pepperoni slices
ced olives

Spray counter lightly with non-stick cooking spray. Combine rolls together and roll into a 13-inch oval pumpkin shape. Place on a sprayed baking sheet. Top with pizza sauce, sausage and cheese.

Bake at 350°F 10-15 minutes. Remove from oven and decorate like a Jack-O-Lantern using green pepper strips, salami and sliced olives. Make a stem out of green pepper and place on top. Return to oven and bake an additional 5-10 minutes.

187

Halloween Handwitches

12 Rhodes™ Dinner Rolls, thawed but still cold
1 egg, beaten
sesame or caraway seeds, if desired
sandwich fillings of your choice

Flatten one roll into a 4x5-inch rectangle. Make 4 equal cuts into one end for fingers, cutting the thumb strip 3/4 of the length of the dough and the finger strips 1/2 the length. Repeat steps for second hand making cuts opposite. Separate the fingers slightly. Pull the thumb strip off to the side and cut in half. Tuck the cut off piece under the palm and press into the dough. Place hands on a sprayed baking sheet. Brush with beaten egg and sprinkle with seeds if desired. Repeat with remaining rolls to make a total of 6 right hands and 6 left hands. Cover with sprayed plastic wrap and let rise 45 minutes or until almost double in size. Remove wrap and bake at 350°F 15-20 minutes or until lightly browned. Use a right hand and a left hand to make a sandwich with the fillin of your choice.

188

Turkey Dinner Rolls

Rhodes Texas™ Rolls
or 2 Rhodes™ Dinner Rolls,
thawed but still cold
egg , beaten
iced almonds, slivered almonds, chopped
cans, pepper corns

Flatten the first roll into a
2 1/2- inch circle for the body
and place on a large sprayed
baking sheet. Cut 1/3 off of
the remaining roll to be
used as a head and neck.
Roll it into a 5-6 inch

drumstick shape and place on one side of body to form a slight curve. Cut head piece
on an angle and pull down against neck to form a wattle. Tuck pointed end under and
slightly flatten for head.

Flatten the rest of the roll into a half circle. Cut 7 long slits to form feathers. Place on
body opposite head and neck. Brush with egg. Place peppercorn on head for eye and
push a slivered almond into the head for a beak. Decorate body and tail with nuts as
desired. Cover with sprayed plastic wrap Let rise 15-30 minutes. Remove wrap and
bake at 350°F 15 minutes or until golden brown.

Christmas Pizza Minis

12 Rhodes™ Dinner Rolls,
  thawed but still cold
flour
pizza sauce
grated mozzarella cheese
red & green peppers, cut into
  small thin strips
pepperoni slices, cut into fourths

Spray counter lightly with non-stick cooking spray. Flatten each roll into a 4 1/2-inch circle. Place circles on sprayed baking sheets. Cover with plastic wrap and let rest 20 minutes. Remove wrap.

Dip 4-inch cookie cutters into flour and cut desired shapes out of each dough circle. Pre-bake at 350°F 8-10 minutes. Remove from oven and let cool.

Top each one with pizza sauce, grated cheese, red and green pepper strips and pepperoni pieces. Bake for an additional 6-8 minutes or until cheese is nicely melted.

Cinnamon Roll Christmas Tree

Rhodes™ Traditional
or AnyTime!™ Cinnamon Rolls
am cheese frosting, included with rolls
ee bits
raschino cherries

Center one roll near the top of a large sprayed baking sheet. Arrange rolls in three more rows 1-inch apart, adding one additional roll to each row, forming a tree. Add two rolls to the bottom to form the trunk. If using Any Time! rolls, bake according to package instructions.

For traditional rolls, cover with sprayed plastic wrap and let rise until double in size. Remove wrap and bake at 350°F 15-20 minutes. When cool, decorate tree with frosting, toffee bits and cherries as desired.

Green Chili Canes

24 Rhodes™ Dinner Rolls,
  thawed to room temperature
2 tablespoons butter, melted
2 cups shredded sharp cheddar cheese
2 cans diced green chiles, drained
1/2 teaspoon garlic salt
grated Parmesan cheese

Spray counter lightly with non-stick cooking spray. Combine 12 rolls together and roll into an 18x12-inch rectangle. Repeat with remaining 12 rolls. Brush both dough rectangles with butter. Combine cheddar cheese, green chiles and garlic salt and sprinkle over one dough rectangle. Top with remaining dough rectangle, butter side down. Cut into twelve 1 1/2-inch strips. Twist each strip several times and turn one end to resemble a candy cane or shepherd's hook. Place at least one inch apart on large sprayed baking sheets. Sprinkle with Parmesan cheese. Bake at 350°F 15-20 minutes or until golden brown.

Frosty the Doughman

3 Rhodes™ Cinnamon Rolls,
  or 3 Rhodes AnyTime!™ Cinnamon
  Rolls, thawed but still cold
cream cheese icing included with rolls
candies, as desired

For bottom section of doughman, place first cinnamon roll on a sprayed baking sheet. Unwind 3-inches of the second roll, cut off and set aside. Place second roll above first.

Unwind 6-inches of the last roll, cut off and set aside. Place this roll for the head. Using some of the cut off dough, shape a hat for the doughman and place above head.

Cover with sprayed plastic wrap and let rise for about 45 minutes (if using AnyTime! Rolls you can omit this step). Remove wrap and bake at 350°F 15-20 minutes, or until golden brown.

Frost with cream cheese icing (included with rolls) and decorate with candies as desired.

Alphabetical Index

ngredient Index

Baking notes

Baking notes

Baking notes